HEAR THESE VOICES

# HEAR THESE VOICES

## Youth at the Edge of the Millennium

by ANTHONY ALLISON

DUTTON CHILDREN'S BOOKS
NEW YORK

The quotation that appears on page xi is from *The Power of Myth*, by Joseph Campbell with Bill Moyers, Doubleday & Company, New York, 1987.

The names of some of the people in this book have been changed to protect their privacy.

*Library of Congress Cataloging-in-Publication Data*

Allison, Anthony.
Hear these voices: youth at the edge of the millennium /by Anthony Allison.
p.   cm.
Summary: Presents case studies of teenagers living with homelessness, prostitution, alcoholism, and neighborhood violence and interviews with staff members from organizations committed to helping teenagers in crisis.
ISBN 0-525-45353-9 (hc)
I. Youth—United States—Case studies—Juvenile literature.   2. Youth—United States—Psychology—Case studies—Juvenile literature. [I. Youth—Case studies.   2. Youth—Services for.]  I. Title.
HQ796.A535   1999   305.235—dc21   98-38464   CIP   AC

Published in the United States 1999 by Dutton Children's Books, a division of Penguin Putnam Books for Young Readers
345 Hudson Street, New York, New York 10014

Designed by Judith Henry

Printed in Italy
First Edition
10 9 8 7 6 5 4 3 2 I

FOR DOMINIQUE DE MENIL

# ACKNOWLEDGMENTS

I would like to acknowledge all of the young people and organizations who gave me their support and trust. Their work with me on *Hear These Voices* made it possible for me to live a dream.

My editor, Karen Lotz, is the person who made this book possible. Her faith, guidance, insight, and tireless patience are among the greatest gifts I have ever received.

I would like to thank Diana Tejada; Amy Wick; Mary Croghin, of East Hampton Business Services; and Vicky Zachelmeyer, for their great work in transcribing the interviews. Thanks to APM Darkroom, Spectra Photo, John Reed Photo, Doug Kunty, and Richard Sampler for all of their photographic support. And thanks to all at Dutton Children's Books, for their efforts.

I am deeply grateful to Todd Cosgrove and the entire Cosgrove family; Dan Cronin; Michael Farrell; Dee Black; Max Weintraub; Coach Ed Petris; Indian Wells; and Fireside.

And lastly I want to say thank you to my mother and sisters and to my wife, Taya, and my three stepchildren, Dash, Caroline, and Max Snow, for all of their love.

Writing these acknowledgments helps me to remember that together we can do what we cannot do alone.

ANTHONY ALLISON
Amagansett, New York

# A NOTE TO THE READER

This is an extraordinary gift that Anthony Allison has brought us: a journey deep into the hearts and minds of others. In their own words, fifteen teenagers describe what living on the edge of adult society is like today for them and for millions of their peers. It's not about technology and the Information Age. It's not about name-brand sneakers, celebrity worship, or portable music players. It's about the basic issues of survival, common to all people in all times: health, safety, food, and shelter. It's also about finding a community of others to love and be loved by.

In this book, you'll meet some remarkable young men who formerly fended for themselves on the streets of Pretoria and Johannesburg, South Africa. Kicked out by their desperately poor and troubled families, these boys—who may have been only eight, ten, eleven years old at the time—are now working hard to get job skills and an education in a local shelter program. You'll also meet a young woman who lives in Denver. Carrie handles two jobs while getting her high school GED and waiting for housing placement. She's never late for work—even though she often has to sleep under a bridge and must wash up in a rest-room sink.

You'll get to know a young man named Daisy as he copes first with the nightmare of testing HIV positive and then with the daily reality of living with AIDS. You'll meet a young woman named Muay, sold into prostitution and sent to Bangkok by her stepfather when she was only ten. Now Muay is training to be an AIDS educator in her home village. Daisy began to speak to high school classrooms throughout the San Francisco Bay Area about disease prevention and self-respect.

You'll be introduced to Ranson, who lives with his grandmother in South Dakota and decides to connect with his Lakota roots partly as a way of remembering to "stay pure"—keeping away from the drugs and alcohol that cripple so many of his relatives and acquaintances. You'll also meet Irina, a native of Kiev, Ukraine. She confronted a life-threatening drug addiction and found a life-saving community with her peers at Narcotics and Alcoholics Anonymous.

Finally, you'll meet two pairs of best friends: Sharon and Caroline from Belfast, Ireland, and Phil and Antonio from the South Bronx, New York City. Bullets and bombs have torn apart their neighborhoods and left behind wasted lives and lost promise. Each of these young people is determined to keep the bloody violence from seeping permanently into his or her own consciousness—all four are taking action, now, to bring about a safer lifestyle for themselves and for their neighbors.

Some of these kids have parents and siblings, and some don't. Some use strong language when they describe their feelings about the dangers they have survived. All have faced the future with determination, and all have sought and found an adult mentor to help them; these mentors add their voices to the book. All are very proud of what they have accomplished. And all have given their trust to Anthony Allison, who respectfully entered their lives, took their pictures, and interviewed them for this book.

Now they're giving their trust to you.

As Antonio says, this book is all about R-E-S-P-O-N-S-I-B-I-L-I-T-Y. If you know someone who should be taking more responsibility for you but isn't, tell him or her about it—or tell another adult you can trust. If you know you should be taking more responsibility for your own actions in some way, follow Irina's lead and take the first step today. And finally, if you're already an adult, we hope you hear how these young people are challenging us to turn our ideals for a better society into reality.

Even if you think you have nothing in common with Daisy or Carrie or Muay, who live on the so-called margins of society, don't be afraid to let their stories change you. It took Anthony Allison more than five years to make this book, and it might take you more than five hours to read it. But neither five hours nor five years is nearly enough time to capture all the promise, purpose, and potential of an individual life: The only way to know what a life can hold is to live it, all the way through.

We hope this book helps you connect with the sense of community that will give us all the courage to live our lives with greater peace and pride—together.

*Furthermore, we have not even to risk the adventure alone, for the heroes of all time have gone before us. The labyrinth is thoroughly known. We have only to follow the thread of the hero path, and where we had thought to find an abomination, we shall find a god. And where we had thought to slay another, we shall slay ourselves. Where we had thought to travel outward, we will come to the center of our own existence. And where we had thought to be alone, we will be with all the world.*

—Joseph Campbell

# PREFACE

We all have had moments in our lives that required us to take risks. This book has its roots in that fact. The risk I had to take was to believe that my life experiences could be used as a way of helping others. More important, for my own peace of mind and survival, I had to find other people who were doing the same thing—so that I could know I was not alone.

*How do I do that?* became the question. This book became the answer.

Even though I had determined what I both wanted and needed, I began the odyssey of making this book with the thought that I would never complete it. You see, up until this point I had not finished much of what I had started in my life. So I went into the project with a great desire but also with a great deal of fear and knowledge about my own past failings. Yet almost as soon as I began working, the pieces began to fall exactly into place; the book started to take on a life of its own. And best of all, the life of the book did not seem willing to let *my* demons of self-doubt get in the way. *What was this strength?* I would ask myself. *Where was it coming from? Why was I experiencing it now, and never before in my life?*

I believe, very strongly, that what brought this project to completion was the incredible trust of the young people you will read about. As they spoke, they addressed the need of all young people to be heard as they transcend specific issues in their lives and come to a new understanding of their own survival: that to help themselves, to keep themselves safe, they have to think and work with others.

Joseph Campbell says in his magnificent book *The Power of Myth* that giving ourselves to some higher end is the ultimate test. He says that the ability to stop thinking about ourselves ahead of others is the "truly heroic transformation of consciousness." And that's what myths deal with—a heroic change in consciousness. As I reread the stories in this book, I realize very clearly that these young people have done that. Some show it in ways that are more obvious than others, but all have gone through powerful transformations in how they interpret their importance not only to themselves, but to others and to the world. I am so lucky to have been a witness to their evolving journeys.

All of the young people were involved in programs, working with individuals who played supportive and motivating roles in their lives. Whether these programs dealt with HIV and AIDS, runaways, homelessness, violence, drugs, or alcohol—and no matter where they were located in the world—I saw common threads in what made them work. Those who worked with the young people paid attention and listened. One might say, "That is so obvious—of course they would do that." But I saw how truly difficult listening can be. To be really present for another person—to listen, to respect a decision that you can understand but still disagree with—that's very difficult. Not to enable, but to empower. To tell someone he is important and that he has something to offer, no matter what. To love someone because she is a human being and for no other reason. To come to terms with the fact that not every person will want your help—and that some, in fact, won't make it, with or without you.

This is the work being done in these programs, and it takes great patience, resilience, strength, and faith. Sadly, so many more are needed. For every one program, we could use ten more. Just as sad is the fact that we all have heard this before.

I had read the quote from Joseph Campbell that appears on page xi in the past but not with a great deal of attention or reaction. It was only after I finished my travels and editing that I came across it once again and was struck immediately. The quote explained exactly what I had hoped the book would become. Now I really knew that the young people I had worked with had given me—and you, the reader—something truly extraordinary. So I ask that as you read along and look at the photographs, try not to compare but to identify—to find a part of yourself within them. By listening to these voices, I hope you will be able to learn more about how you live, not only as an individual, but with others in the community of man.

ANTHONY ALLISON

# CONTENTS

*page 79*

## RAPID CITY, SOUTH DAKOTA

Ranson, 14 years old

*page 119*

## BELFAST, NORTHERN IRELAND

Sharon, 14 years old
Caroline, 14 years old

*page 97*

## KIEV, UKRAINE

Irina, 18 years old

*page 145*

## SOUTH BRONX, NEW YORK CITY

Phil, 17 years old
Antonio, 18 years old

HEAR THESE VOICES

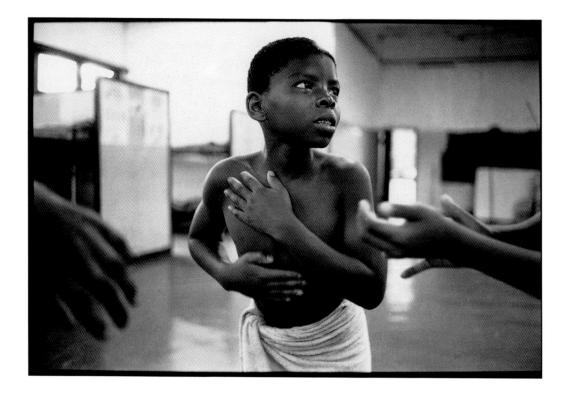

# THE BOYS OF STREETWISE

ages 10 to 19 years

**Sunrise, blue sky, rain, storms, lightning, dusk, sunset, stars, the moon. It was all there, every day that I spent with the boys who lived at the Streetwise Shelter in Johannesburg and those who came by the drop-in center in Pretoria. Luckily for me, I had a lot of days to spend.**

## SHEPARD/13 years old

One day, four years ago, I was living with my mother and my grandmother, and we moved to live with my other father. I don't know my real father. I've never met him. I don't even know what I would say to him. So, in this new place, my other father say he is hungry, and I must give him food. He get mad at me, and after that, he kick the fires on the stove. The house is on fire. I run out with my little sisters and my big sister. One boy, my little brother, was left inside, and he closed the door and the fire gets him. Then he go to the hospital and he dies. He was seven years. My mother says that I killed him. I don't know why. I am angry at my mother because it feels sad. I love him; I love my brother.

I had difficult times living with my mother after my brother passed away. My mother would get mad and beat me at night and then tell me to go sleep outside. She also would tell me to go and look for clothes. I came to the streets at twelve years old, and I lived on the streets for four months. I am thinking that if I had just had my father, I would never have come to the street.

People see us on the streets right before they go home and see their own children. These people think that we children run away from home and come to the street because all we want to do is smoke glue. That's not true.

Some people are nice. They give us clothes, or some money to buy some food and something to sleep with. I would park cars or sometimes wash cars to make money. Then the police helped me. They found us in the street and said: Come here. We come and they say: Get inside the car. And we go inside, and they take us here, to the Streetwise Shelter. I have been at Streetwise for seven months.

When I was in the street, my mother did not come to look for me. I would have. I don't think my mother likes me. She has problems. She is drinking, and then beats us. Parents should sit down and help each other, or at least have people come to teach them how to live better with their children. I want to tell my mother that I love her, and I would love to stay with her. But I would not go back to live with her until she gets the person who can help her solve her problem.

If you stay on the street, you're going to get into trouble. It happens. You will sniff glue and maybe steal things. But now if you're in the shelter, you're going to school. You won't sniff glue, because you're going to get food and everything else that they can give. I feel better now because I'm in the shelter. People are not cruel to me, and nobody says: Go fetch me some glue. And nobody says: Go sleep outside. You feel loved here. That makes me have hope.

I believe in me, because I like it when I go to school. If I work hard, I know I will succeed, and I'll get what I need. I want to work as a social worker, since I'm living in the city now. I still feels a hurting, seeing the other boys staying at the shelter rather than being with their parents.

All my sisters live in Soweto. They live with a friend of my mother. I saw them not too long ago. We played ball. When I saw them, it was so much fun. I feel pain in the heart because I see some other children with both fathers and mothers.

# DUMISANI/15 years old

At home, we are four. I saw my mother this year. We stayed together for just a short period. I asked her, "Is everything okay?" and she say, "Yes, okay." Then my mother changed, and she started telling me that I must go back to the Streetwise Shelter and tell them that they must keep me forever because I am a poison, a snake, and she doesn't want me anymore. First I goes around and stays with people that I doesn't know, but she says I must not come home, because I will poison my brother and sisters. So I go back to the shelter. I believe that my mother really doesn't care.

Sometimes when I draw, my mother says I must forget drawing or wanting to be an artist because it makes me go crazy. But I think God gave me the talent of being an artist. My mother says a lot of stuff, and I cannot keep on carrying it around in my head. My father, too. I don't see him; he doesn't help. He only drinks. Maybe people with families like us, people who came to the streets, could just have a person tell their parents what good people their children are.

Once when I was in the street, a man abused me. I was playing a little game at the shop he was near. The man came and chased me and beat me, telling me my

▲ *Shepard (above)*

5

mother didn't teach me anything. He kept kicking me until the blood came up in my ear. Since the boys on the streets are little, see, the police should be taking care of these guys. The police should take them to schools to learn what is happening on the streets. It's very dangerous. Sometimes there is people selling drugs so they would have some money. One time, two white people came to us and showed us a gun they purchased so that we would run away. It is very dangerous on the streets. The police should start caring for the children.

▲ *Dumisani, Ronnie, Peter (above)*

Some boys don't want to stay in the shelter. They are used to life on the street; they think it's their life, and they enjoy it, and the street is their home. They don't want to be given something like an education. They enjoy what they have, like glue and cigarettes. I stay at the shelter because I want to go to school and have a future. I want to be a good person when I am older, and I don't want to be staying on the street. People call us street children; we will grow up on the street with them calling us street brothers or street elders, and in the end they are calling us street fathers. So I don't want to look like that, and I don't want to have people call me such things.

## RONNIE/14 years old

**W**hen I was thirteen, I run away with a friend to the street, and I stay there for a month or more. I never dream of anything on the street that was good, except that maybe one person would help me one day. I know when I was living on the street, some people passing by will maybe give me a piece of food. I was afraid that if I gets hit by a car, no one would know where I comes from, and I would end up with no one knowing where I am. Sometimes I'm sorry I left home because it was cold in the street.

I left when my mother started telling me to go get the water. I was staying in a shed with my mother, and I always does it, but I didn't like it, so I stopped getting the water. Then my mother beat me for this. My mother is the reason I don't want to stay at home for good. If I goes home and stays with my mother, I would like her to get my elder brother, in the other town, to come and help me with the water.

Me and the boys on the street talk about it sometimes—what made us go away from home. We not talk that much about it, because we will keep on thinking about it and it won't make us feel right. I haven't talked about it with the boys at the shelter yet.

I came here to Streetwise because I thought they would help me and give me food and a place to stay. I can wash myself and my clothes and go to school. After school, I would like to be a doctor, yes, a doctor, and when I grow up I will help other people. When I see the children on the street, I thinks that some of them will come here and stay at the shelter and stop smoking glue cigarettes. If they build more shelters and go out and take those boys still on the street and bring them in, that will help.

## MANDISIA/15 years old

**M**y father beat me, and when he was drunk, he would beat me more and tell me that I am not his son. The last time my father was beating me it was about 2 A.M., and he didn't use a belt, he use a wire. My father is an electrician. This time I left home. I took a train to a town

and met some guy there, and I followed him until he came to Johannesburg.

I use to run away before and sometimes go to relatives. My mother would come to get me. She would start by phoning the relatives, trying to find me. When the phones were out, she would go there and tell them that she was looking for me. When she gets me, we would talk, and she'd ask me why I left. You see, my father beats me when my mother is not around. My mother would go into the bedroom of my relatives, and they'll speak, and then from there they'll accompany my mother

and me to my father, and they would speak to him.

What I want to say to my father is: Why is he saying that I'm not his son? Maybe that is what makes him feel like beating me. Truly, if you think that I'm not your son, do you feel like beating me?

Sometimes I do feel like I'm important, but sometimes, when my father beat me until I couldn't see, I thought to kill myself. I was thinking that I was the only one who suffer like this. But the other boys at the shelter have suffered. Sometimes we talk, but when I think of asking other boys, I thinks that some of them will feel pain when they talk about their experiences and their past. I doesn't want to make them to feel angry at themselves and to feel pain.

## PETER/14 years old

Hello; my name is Peter. I am the firstborn in my family. I have one sister and four brothers. At home, I only get one slice of bread to eat, so that made me feel angry. Sometimes I would go to the neighbors and ask for food. There was a big house next to my place, and sometimes we would call, and they would give us food and clothes. We would carry the golf clubs for the whites who play golf there so they will give us money. Then I would buy bread and stay under the big rooms at the club, and we will eat the bread. Another thing to do is get bottles, lots of bottles, and sell them to get money. Sometimes with the money I would buy sugar, bread, and tea for my family at home. My dream is that I want to own my own shops that sell food.

My friend and I was playing a game called Stop. It's when the train moves out of the station and you jump on. It's fun. When you get hurt, it's not fun. One time on the trains, we were caught without tickets by the police, and we were taken to a kitchen where they made us wash pots. And it happened one time that we were playing on trains that came to Johannesburg. So we took it and never went home. That's when we started sleeping on the streets. We went to a church and then they bring me to Streetwise. Six months I've been here.

My family needs help with things. Needs it bad. My mother and me, we used to stay from house to house. My mother drinks the homemade beer, and I don't actually know where she lives now; it's somewhere in Pretoria. My father I do not know. My mother I think loves me. Sometimes when she has some money, she buys me sweets.

Sometimes I stayed in the mines. Later, I stays with my grandmother and my three uncles who are staying with their girlfriends. They love me, but I don't think they care what happens to me. With them I was okay. I'm happy to stay with them, but the only thing is, I would get very little to eat. My uncles have no work, and my grandmother is a pensioner. My grandmother didn't send me to school because she couldn't pay for the school uniform. I will go back to them at Christmas, but I will not stay. If I stay, I will suffer, so instead I will come back to Streetwise and be with these boys. We are happy to live together and know each other. We are friends.

## JOEL / 14 years old

I have one sister and maybe four or five brothers. My father has a job as a bus driver. My mother and father separated, so then I was staying with my father and stepmother. My stepmother is the one that beat me. My stepmother drinks and was beating me, so I ran away. I know this is not right. What is all right is to just live okay like other children. Maybe it's because she is drinking.

What makes me want to stay in the shelter is that I am having the school. I know I am clever and can do better than I does now if I can just go to school. If you don't go to school, you get lost along the way. So I hate to be at home. At the YMCA school, they remind us that if we meet other children who are from a formal school, and they know we are from this school, we mustn't be insulted. We must be able to have our heads up.

# ELVIS/17 years old

My mother used to like Elvis Presley's songs, so she told my father they can make my name to be Elvis. I don't sing, not like Elvis [laughing]. My mother and father live together.

I first came to the town on the weekends with my friend. He was teaching me how to make money parking and washing the cars. So if I made money, I went home, and when money finish I came back into town. I sometimes didn't get enough money to go back home, so I started sleeping in town. My parents came to look for me when I was in the streets. They found me two times, and after that they didn't find me again. When I stayed at home, they didn't do nothing for me. I wanted them to buy me clothes, some shoes. I needed the help. They do have the money, but they don't want to use it. They just keep it in a bucket. They only like to help with money if I'm in school.

I lived on the streets for two and a half years. Now

▲ *Elvis (above)*

11

I've gone back home to live, because I'm the biggest child. If I stay forever in town, who's to help take care of my mother and brothers and sister? They must eat, you see? So, I come in every day and I work with the cars, I get money, and in the afternoon I go home.

I think I should be in school because school is important. The last time I was in school was two years ago. I wish I could go back, because the years are coming now, and you'll never get a job without an education. I was talking with Virginia at Streetwise, and she told me that if I need something for school, I must come to her and she'll help me.

Sleeping on the street is dangerous. People trouble you, start kicking you, swearing at you, and chasing you.

These people who do this, I don't think they got children. If they got children, they not supposed to do that.

Most of the boys on the street, they had problems in home and came to town. Some of them just came to town to work for money, like me.

# WILLIAM/19 years old

I first came onto the street when I was a young boy. My father beat me and told me: You can go to the town. I told him I couldn't go; he said: Yes, you can. We come

▲ *William is interviewed on television about Streetwise (above).*

on the train into town, and in town we find Streetwise. Melinda was working then, and she took us to the church. Then I was fourteen or fifteen years old. That was the last time I went to school. At the church, they started to teach us how to work with our hands, to use lead, to make shoes, repairs, things like that. They was teaching us, and then something terrible happened. People—it was three white men—burned down the church. I jumped. Other boys jumped. Seven of the small boys were killed in the fire.

My mother died in 1988; my father died in 1994. My father sometimes would go to a job, find a little bit of work—three weeks to five weeks of pay. But we were very suffering for food. Sometimes for three days we were not eating. I would go do something, rob money, or maybe steal something to eat or cook.

I hope it is not too late for me because of no real school and little work. Okay, listen: The thing is, I waste my time. I waste my time, and now I think I'm too old to go back to school. I left school when I was fifteen. I was clever at school. I think now it is too late to go. You have to work when you are older. I think I can make money and help my grandmother. I'm a man in my home now. I must look after my grandmother and my sister.

About these boys on the street: what I want to do is to try to talk to them. The small boys, they can understand me when I tell them they must stop using glue. I know glue, and using glue is not the right thing. It can make you crazy and your mind upset, you know? And you fight each other, and you can take something like a knife and stick each other, and it can kill you. Sometimes when I try to tell them to stop using glue, they tells me, "You're not parents; you are not my mother, you are not

my father, you are nothing of my family." But I try, yes I do. I say, "The thing is I love you, and I don't want you to be crazy or something like that. Please stop glue, and you mustn't be fighting."

One day I woke up, I walked out with David from Streetwise, and I went to the shops where they are selling glue because I know which shops. I walk in and tell them they must stop selling glue to the small guys. So one of the men says, "You can't stop my business. I don't call a boy from the street to tell him he must come to buy glue. That boy come for himself to buy glue. I make a business, and you can't stop my business."

In Sunnyside, there are seven stores selling the glue. We went to all of them. One of them they told me "Yes, we will stop selling glue." That is the first shop that I know that can understand. Maybe I will try to talk to Mandela [laughing] so he can make a meeting with the policemen, and then they must talk to the stores. These peoples, they must stop selling to the boys the glue.

## PHILLIP/16 years old

I am going to go back home as soon as I can. I have some money, and soon this is Christmas, so I want to end the year with my mother and my family. I want to listen to my mother and my grandmother, so I can hear what they're going to tell me about next year. I want to change my life and go back to school. I think I am going to try observing the rules of my mother. It will be interesting. The woman who have bring me into this world is now really suffering about me. She thought when she brings me in, she thought she was going to have a little boy, a beautiful boy that will observes rules; now the boy

she did bring in the world is no longer a boy, but a man who is still sleeping in the street.

Last night when we were walking I saw something I had never seen before. I saw two white men fighting. Yes, that is true. I had never seen a white person fighting with his brother. I had only seen blacks fighting blacks, or whites fighting blacks. Yeah, we fight too much, and because of this maybe we hate each other. Maybe I hate you because you have money. I don't have money—that's why I hate you, see? So I fight you, and then in a way that's how it all started. Blacks are fighting every day, right? Even now when you go out and ask who is fighting, they

will show you black people which are fighting. Some blacks are very stupid persons because they are fighting with their hands, or with guns—killing each other. So what they have to do is fight with mouth and discussing these things. To fight is just a foolish thing. We don't have to do this.

I was born into a suffering house, and I mustn't suffer my whole life. I know that. I know that I have friends to help me, and those boys on the street, we must give them a hope that if they can live and live right, they are going to be beautiful boys. When you give these boys the hope, I don't think we're going to suffer so much death.

▲ *Phillip (above)*

The street children in South Africa, like those in other parts of the world, come mostly from poor families. In South Africa, the poorest people are nonwhite people. This is partly because from 1948 to 1993, South Africa had an apartheid system of government. Apartheid means "separateness," and the idea was that people from each race group in the country should live apart from each other. The areas set aside for white people were the best of all. The education program for white children was better, and well-paid jobs were kept for white people only. Nonwhite children who were found to be in need of care because their parents beat or neglected them did not have equal rights. There were more children's homes for white children than for nonwhite children, even though they numbered about one-fifth as many.

Because children and their families were often hungry, and there was no money for school fees and clothes, many thought it would be better to leave home to find work so they could help their families or get a good education for themselves. Sometimes mothers even asked their eldest children to leave home, even if they were only ten or eleven years old. After working on the streets for a time, many children would decide not to go back home anymore. Adults who were unhappy and bitter because they could not find jobs often drank to escape from their problems, and many then beat and swore at their children day after day. So more children ran away to the streets, not just to help their families, but because of the many angry adults who, if they did not have so many problems, might have been better parents.

When the ANC (African National Congress) came to power in South Africa, and Mandela became president of the country, he made a speech about how the country's street children needed special help. Despite this, many people, including some in the new government, still want to take all the street children and put them into institutions and reformatories where nobody can see them. They seem to think it is more important for tourists and shoppers not to see dirty children hanging around the streets than it is for the children to be truly helped.

Many of the children we're talking about have never used a telephone or a refrigerator or ridden in a car. They may not know what an ice cube or a hammer is, or a map. Many do not know what the world is.

We need to help families sort out their problems so that children can go home again. It would be wonderful if all adults could be given good jobs, but this is hard, since many cannot read or write. At Streetwise, we find that giving food every month, or putting families in touch with churches and other places that collect clothes and offer friendly support, makes peoples' lives more comfortable. When they see that someone cares about them, it helps build up their dignity. They are then more willing to agree that they have a problem in looking after their children and to learn better ways of parenting. Most people do care about their children, but do not know how to escape the trap of hurting them in anger. They can be taught how to do this, or other relatives can be found who will take the children into their own families. Even though sorting out family problems takes time and money, it is much less expensive than keeping a child in an institution that he or she hates.

We also urgently need to teach street children in South Africa about drug abuse and to help those who have started to use drugs. Although many have sniffed glue or other things to make them feel good, to stop hunger pain, or to feel sleepy when they want to shut out the hard outside world, they usually are able to stop doing these things quite easily. Starting really in 1993, drug dealers have been pouring drugs into the country and selling them on the streets. The street children do not get to see the programs on television or attend school programs on drug abuse. They are an easy target for those dealers who offer lots of money to anyone who will carry their

▲ *Streetwise boys of Pretoria (above)*

drugs for them. These children do not realize what drugs can do to them if they use them, and they also don't realize how strongly they can be punished if they are caught with drugs.

Education is the key. Many people, especially children who complain about having to go to school every day, are surprised at how thirsty street children are for education. Teachers are surprised by the eagerness of street children to learn anything and everything they can. One teacher at Streetwise could hardly believe it when a ragged boy of about ten years told her, "You are talking too much. We want to learn. When are we going to do some work?" Most people don't realize that most street children don't plan to stay on the streets all their lives.

They want homes and jobs and families who will never have to live on the streets. They believe that education will help them achieve this.

It is extremely difficult to teach children when they live on the streets. They are tired and hungry or high from glue. Many fall asleep in the middle of a lesson. People are afraid when they see lots of dirty, ragged children in parks. They may not notice that they are having lessons. If they think that the children are getting together to rob them or to vandalize buildings, they call the police to take them away. It is impossible to relax and enjoy your lessons when you are always afraid of being arrested.

Street children manage to get money for food and clothes by begging and doing odd jobs such as washing cars, carrying shopping bags, and sweeping pavements. Because they work with money every day, they can add and subtract and multiply and divide very quickly. But they don't know they are clever at this, because nobody ever tells them so. Apart from food, street children need love and space and a chance to develop their personal skills. Although they show a tough face to the world, they long to be loved and cared for, and they believe that education will give them a chance at a dignified future.

▲ *Boys asleep on the street in Pretoria (above)*

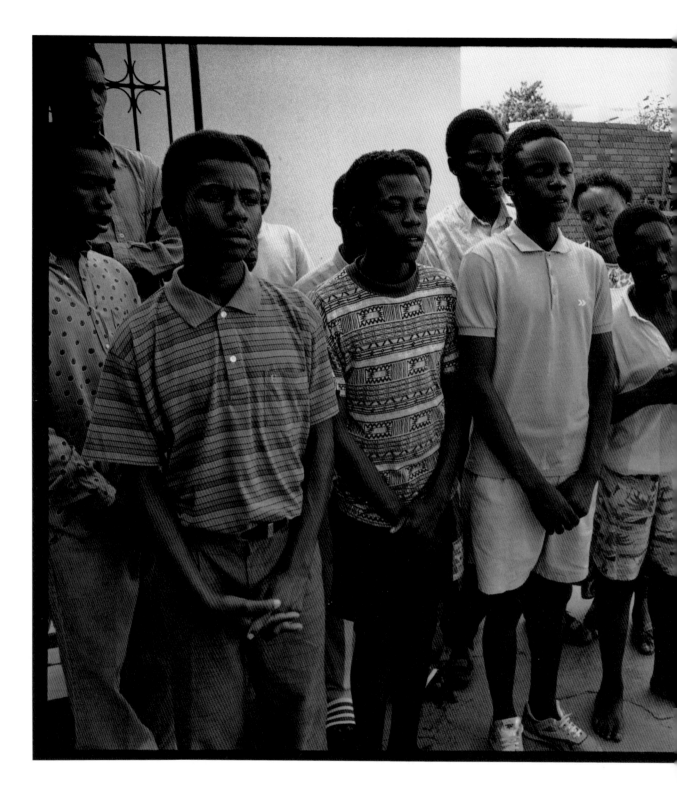

THE BOYS OF STREETWISE

## MOLATLHEGI MASHISHI / branch coordinator of Streetwise in Pretoria

In the past, children who were in the streets encountered a lot of problems with the police. They were beaten up, sometimes taken to faraway places and left there to walk back to town with very swollen feet. Things are better now, but it still happens to a certain extent. The police also were after those of us who were working with these children. They didn't want us to be too involved, because they said we encouraged children to come to the streets by helping them. When we would report a case of assault on one of the boys by the police to the police, then they would be after us all the time. There was also the possibility for them even to kill you. It wasn't safe to work for political reasons: it was taking chances.

When I see the boys out on the street, it makes me sad. We don't have enough facilities and resources to actually help all these boys. I start to think humanity is no more, because people used to care for each other, and now we are losing that humanity little bit by little bit. A lack of care from a lot of people—it's a problem. I think what these poor boys need to heal their wounds is love, a lot of love. They need a place where they can be cared for. These boys are very brave. Their bravery is that they can forgive; yes, some of them find it not so difficult and can forgive and continue to work hard on things. They are doing their best; they are brave. So it is important for me to see and feel this, because you know, it makes me work harder. I see myself when I'm helping these boys. It means a lot to help somebody.

◄ *Streetwise Shelter in Johannesburg (left)*

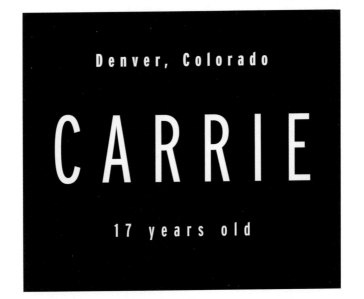

Denver, Colorado

CARRIE

17 years old

Since she was about twelve, Carrie has been running away from home or has been in the government system of foster homes and other placements. When I first met her, she was homeless in Denver, getting help from Urban Peak—a group that works with homeless and runaway youth—and trying to sort out her life.

I don't know if anybody could ever understand what it's like out here. My best friend back in Indiana, she doesn't understand. She's like, oh, man, she doesn't have a new enough car, she doesn't have the newest clothes that just came out. I'm like, what are you talking about? You live in this wonderful house, and you have everything I could possibly dream of, and you still aren't satisfied. What if you were to do without your basics that people need in life, I mean just like a friend, someone to show you affection. You know what I'm saying? It's hard for her to understand.

## Family and Running Away

When I was born, I lived only with my grandmother. Then my father took me for a couple years, then I moved back with my grandma, and I stayed there. I didn't start going back and forth between my grandma and my father until I was eleven or thirteen.

My mother doesn't live in Gary. I've talked to her before, but it's not like anything special. The last time I spoke with her was about eight months ago. I guess it was all right. I just—I don't know, I just don't like her. I don't really have any relationship with her. Never have. She's got a boyfriend she been with for seventeen years. She's paralyzed from the waist down. So she been with him and they all happy 'n' stuff, which I guess is cool.

Sometimes she try to include me, but she just act like I'm supposed to love her, like she's s'posed to be my mom. That ain't my mom; I don't have one.

My father used to say he wished I was never born. I don't think he care about me. I sometimes wish he could get a house. Maybe he'd change, but that ain't never happened. He hustles to make his money. From day to day, he just kinda does whatever.

When I was thirteen, my father turned me over to the state because I was out of control. I just didn't want to be at home. I was running away, fighting—they

▲ *Staying with friends in a rented room (above)*

thought I was crazy. My grandmother's real religious, right? And she tried to get me to go to church, and I didn't want to, and it was a big ol' battle. So I would just run, really to nowhere, just to the streets. I wouldn't even stay at friends' houses. It got to the point where I just ran so the police or whoever would take me away.

One night my father even helped me run away. It was cold outside, but he just tell me, "Get your ass up there." He told me where to go and then called the police and told 'em I ran. They still didn't do nothing—they brought me back home.

I think I was about twelve when I went to my first foster home. I've been in three foster homes, and I ran

away from those. I would just run back home. My father wouldn't do nothing when I got there. Things would be cool, for a minute, and then it would just be more problems. After my last foster home, I went to some placements. Group homes. This was all around the neighborhood of Gary, Indiana. Then I got sent to this program in Maine, from not being able to succeed anywhere, you know. I ended up graduating from there and went back home. I was home for not even a few days, and me and my grandmother got into it.

I just didn't want to be with my family. So I started getting into trouble and messing up and put myself back into the system. That was all my doing. I went to another hospital, in Chicago, so they could evaluate me and find another placement. And that's how I first came out to Denver. They sent me here for nine months to the Excelsior, which is an all-girls school, and that's one place I hate. I hated it. The only justice they did me was giving me a different outlook on wanting to go to school, wanting to learn.

During all this time, do you know how I felt about myself and my family and the world? Like shit. I didn't feel safe anywhere. I was afraid of everything—going home, being locked up, being by myself, everything. I just thought about leaving and living in the streets and making it on my own. But it's not easy to do that, and at first

I really didn't survive. The first time I got in trouble out on the streets, I went back home. I didn't know what else to do. When I would run away, I wasn't looking for nothing, except I just wanted a normal life and I just wanted to have a family. I wished things could be better.

## Coming to Denver

I left Gary because I couldn't get away from the insanity there, no matter what I did. So I moved out to a different city nearby, and I was living with this woman rent-free and watching her kids during the day. She was really cool; she also hooked me up with another job. We even went out and partied. I felt happy, I was doing this 'n' that, but I was going insane. I couldn't stand watching three kids every day and going to work. I got so sick of it. I didn't feel like I was giving myself any kind of anything.

Since I didn't have nothing to tie me down, my decision on coming to Denver was made in less than twenty-four hours. Everybody told me, "I did the same stuff you're doing now, running from everybody, thinking you're going to make it better, but you're not, you're gonna come back here feelin' sorry for yourself and have everyone take care of you." I said to them, "That's bullshit. You don't know me. I don't care what 'chall say."

My intention in coming out to Denver was to put my life together. I wanted to get my GED, to get a job, and to get away from the violence back in my neighborhood. I knew that Urban Peak could help with some of that. When I first got to Denver, I was a little leery for a couple a weeks. I knew about the night shelter, but I had a hard time finding it at first. I stayed there four or five days, but I didn't like having to come in at a certain time. I was new to Denver again, and I wanted to know what was happenin'. I felt like I was missin' out on something [laughing]—what, I don't know.

So I just left and started livin' in the tunnels. Then the first day I went back to Urban Peak to see Adams; I was with this girl, and she was like, "Just kick it with me, let's go somewhere, do something." And that day I got a job. So I went back to the shelter to have a place to sleep and take a shower.

Whenever I'm sleeping outside somewhere, I just get up, and if it's not too late, I'll go to a friend's house and take a shower or I'll come to Urban Peak for one. If not, then I'll just go to work and wash up there, so I look halfway presentable. I take everything with me—soap, washcloth, towel, toothbrush, everything. I wash my hair in the bathroom sink.

After work, I think about where I'm sleeping. If I'm by myself, like now, I just kinda hang out in the streets as late as I can to see if I run into anybody I know and try to hook up and kick it with them. Sometimes I'll just meet people right off the street; they'll be, "Where you goin'? Whatcha doin' tonight?" They'll be like, "Come back to my place." I don't know them, but it's a place to stay. Sometimes it's safe; sometimes it's not. If I'm desperate enough, I'll do it anyway. But if not, and worse comes to worse, I'll just go to the tunnels, or to the bridge. I try not think about it until I have to. People at work ask me about it. They're like, "Where you goin' tonight?" I'm like, "I don't know until I get there." I'm very impulsive. Very.

I don't think people think about safety with all this unless they're really looking at reality. Really the hardest part of living on the street is people judging you, like you ain't shit, like you'll never be shit. But I know that I wanna be something.

Lately I've been staying at my friend Kevin's house, but everybody's been drunk, everybody's been fighting; people getting into it constantly, police coming up in there and kicking everybody out. It's been crazy. I'm comfortable, because I'm used to being around it. To a certain degree, it makes me feel good, 'cause I feel like I know what's going on. Even though these people ain't really my friends. To them, all I am is just another bitch or ho. Even though I'm not. But that's how they categorize you, you know what I'm saying? But at least it's somebody to talk to, who come from that way that I know. When I came out here, for a long time I didn't even meet people who was into that gangsta lifestyle. So it's easy to stay out of it, but the first set of people I meet that's into it, it's hard as hell to get out, to like, leave.

I ain't going to give up, though. There are days when I feel like it. But before I leave this state, I will accomplish my GED, even if it takes me five years. That is one thing I came here to do, and that is one thing I will leave here finished. School I like a lot. And I've done some other good things for myself. I've never missed a day of work. Tomorrow night after work, I think I'm probably going to go out with Lisa, my boss. She said she would help me study my writing. She wants to. She's been telling me, "We've got to go study sometime before you take your test."

Urban Peak has helped me out to a certain degree. They ain't got me no job, and they really ain't done nothing to help me get my GED. But they just set me straight in my thinking, helping me figure out what I really want and what is really important to me. Then I can do it for myself. Sometimes Adams just kinda helps me set it straight.

## Leaving Kevin's

Tonight I'm going to wash my clothes, which means getting my things out of Kevin's house. I've got to get out of there. I can feel trouble about to happen, and I just don't want to be involved. It's hard, because I'm scared, like something's going to happen to me. See, I didn't tell you this, but probably I should have. Brian asked me the other day if I wanted to rent a place and pay half, and I was like yeah, sure. As long as it's just me and you, and you don't have all this crazy shit going on. But now I don't want to, and I don't know how to tell him, 'cause I think he'll go off on me. I've only known Brian probably not even a week, and I don't want to live with him. I don't feel safe. But I just kinda been keeping that to myself, 'cause I was dumb. I didn't exactly tell him I wanted to live with him. I just sort of let him think that I would. It wouldn't be so bad to have a place to just chill and hang out. But I know it's best for me not to do it, and I don't plan to. So I just gotta get my stuff outta there before his day to move, and I just won't see him. Then I'll be like, "Man, I haven't seen you around." You understand?

See, I'm in the Transitional Living Program [TLP], waiting to get a placement in one of the apartments. It's frustrating because it's taken so long. They told me it'd be max about two months, and that I should sign up right away—that people move up, move out. But by November, it'll be four and a half months I've been waiting. I believe sometimes that things will get better, but how

long do I have to wait for the good to come? I always expect the bad to come; it's cool, you know, you don't wait on that. But waiting on the good takes forever.

## Getting the Gun

I bought a gun, because when I go home to visit, I want to retaliate against people that done me wrong before. Like the dude, you know, the dude who raped me and all his friends who helped him. The ones who made me do things I didn't want to do. I would feel like I got justice, because the police won't do nothin' to them.

▲ *After spending the night under a bridge, Carrie leaves to go first to Urban Peak and then to work (above).*

I know I could get away with it. That could happen in my city with no problem. The police don't care. The police are smokin' crack. You give 'em a couple sacks of dope, and it's like poof! I didn't see that. Nobody cares. All it's gonna be to them is just another black man dead, and they're not gonna say, "Oh, this white girl killed him." So if I find those people, I'll have no hesitation. I don't think I'll have any feelings of being scared. Probably later on, I might feel bad, but that's just for taking a person's life, not the person I took, but just in general a person. But eventually I would make it back.

Having the gun here in Denver scares me. I thought with a gun, I could feel hard. You know what I'm saying? Like you got some heart. Ain't nobody going to step on

you once they know you got a gun. But it's not about having it, it's about using it, and whether you got enough guts. Here in Denver I really don't have no enemies, and I'm more scared somebody might use it against me or that I'm gonna get caught with it.

## Misconceptions about Homeless and Runaway Youth

Out on the street, sometimes it seems like you just entered a dark world. You can't rely on nobody but yourself. You gotta take what you can get. When I first came out to Denver, I couldn't take a shower, couldn't change my clothes, couldn't see a doctor, couldn't do anything. Couldn't eat. I mean, it's horrible. A lot of people misjudge homeless youth and try to categorize us. You see them looking at young people who panhandle, and they're like, "Oh my God, look at that!" People think that's all we're ever going to be. Or they're like, "Yeah, you just want to get something to drink or some drugs." A lot of the time they put it like that on TV and the newspapers, like all the homeless and youth do all day is get high or something like that.

I don't use drugs. I drink beer sometimes. But what about all these businesspeople that get up in here with all that? People don't want to talk about them. People know,

▲ *Trying to get her clothes back from the apartment she and some friends had taken over temporarily—no luck today (above)*

but they don't want to know. They don't mind if we look bad, because we're the so-called lowlife. If you got a bad life, people think that all you can do is get high. But look at the preps and jocks at school—they all doin' that stuff. And they're what people consider ideal kids. What I need money for, it's like, "Man, I'm hungry. I want to eat. I really, really do." Or it's been a week and a half since I had a shower, and I just wish I could take a shower.

For people who ain't been out here, it's hard to understand. They got the keys to their house; they can lock it. Ain't nobody comes in unless you say so. You got a shower, you go to the bathroom when you want to go,

you get up when you want, regardless of your responsibilities—it's all your choice. You got money in your pocket, if you want to eat out. If you don't, that's cool, you eat in. You know what I'm saying?

I can offer something to people who think about coming to the street. I've already been there, and I'll explain to them the ropes, you know, warn 'em about what's ahead of them, good and bad. I'll tell them that it's not going to all make sense till they get there. I didn't understand, either, when I was in that situation, and I remember people trying to tell me where I was going to end up—going through the system, placement after placement in juvenile detention. But the only people telling me that was my father, and other older people, and they really didn't understand. If one of my homies was to tell me, I'd probably consider it more. There's been a lot of things that I wanted to do that woulda gotten me in lots of trouble, but they'd tell me, "It ain't cool."

It's kind of like hitchhiking. It's cool for a minute, it's exciting, you got your adrenaline rushing and shit, but you always gotta watch you don't get with a crazy person. 'Cause I've been with a few crazy truck drivers, and I been with some cool ones. And once you been with a cool one, you forget; you think everyone else is like that. But one day you will have a bad trip, so you always gotta be on edge. Don't ever be trusting.

I tell the people that I kick it with, don't trust me. Not because I'm untrustworthy, but if you think you can trust me, then you'll start thinking you can trust somebody else. You just don't trust nobody—even the people you hang out with. I don't want to consider myself hard, but if you ain't like completely down, if you're not willing to take a bullet, those people'll just mess you up. If I was telling somebody else, I'd rather her kinda know what's up. It's not always pretty.

## What Can Be Done to Help

They need shelters, more shelters—more that are open all day, every day. Urban Peak is good. But if you stay at their night shelter, and that's part of their help, you get kicked out in the morning at seven o'clock. Then you don't have nowhere to go until eleven, when they open up Urban Peak. And you can't go to Urban Peak on the weekends. If you're new to the game, then it's hard, those mornings and the weekend.

I also don't think you can always tell people: Do more or get out. That ain't gonna stop the problem. Plus the night shelter is only a thirty-day shelter, so what are they telling you? If you don't get your shit together in thirty days, we're putting you out. Regardless if someone don't want to do anything, I think they should be able to have a place to stay. There should be some restrictions, but I would never say to put someone in the street, even if they're not gonna go to school and not gonna go to work.

What you can say is: If you're not doing school or work, then while you're here you're gonna do such 'n' such. You know? That's fair. Then if people are like, "Well, I'm not staying there because I don't want to do it," then they're putting their own self on the street. For me, it's not hard to follow the rules. For me, everything is what it's about and who it's comin' from.

In Gary, there was nobody really to go to. Not really. They don't have services like this. I called around. I called Chicago a lot to see if they had shelters that would take me. But you had to be a ward of Illinois, even though I was like, "But I really need help." I called the runaway hotline, saying, "You got to help me; I can't be here no more. Can you put me somewhere where I can get this straightened out?" But they couldn't do nothing. It was such a low-income neighborhood in a low-income state, and we don't have the services. The help they had was not going to help me.

## An Apartment of Her Own

I don't think my friends are going to be different with me if I get an apartment with TLP. They would only look at me different if I ignored them, like I was better

than them 'cause I had a place to stay now and they didn't. But see, I'm not like that. I would never turn my back on them. They were there for me, you know what I'm saying? Through thick 'n' thin. But my only real friends are Creeper and Forty and Sprocket, and they already gave me a place to stay when they had it. Why wouldn't I return the favor? They couldn't live up in here, but they more than welcome to come stay a couple nights whenever they need to through my eighteen months, take a shower, you know, sit down and grub. They could stay there until two o'clock in the morning.

I don't know if they would use me as an example of moving forward. I don't know if they think that way. It's

possible, but I don't think they respect me a lot. I mean, I think I can offer them something. I know that Creeper 'n' them, if they could take a shower every day, if they had a place where they could keep their stuff without it getting stolen, they'd probably be farther along than where they are right now. And I'm more than willing to do that for them if they want to.

## Moving On and Looking Back

**I went to see Carrie again three months later, bringing some pictures with me.**

Well, I finally got my apartment through TLP. Got a new job and I got my GED. Looking at these photos, it's like the circle of my life. I'm amazed that I'm finally through it. But now that I made it here, sometimes I kinda forget. I think, "That's not really as bad as things were." As soon as you get to where you want, you're so happy you try not to remember. When I look at the pictures, I can remember the feelings, but I don't feel the same way now. It changes. I'm finally getting everything I want in my life.

I'm happy about me and my father getting along better. With all the things that happened between us—if something does happen to him, and we're on good terms, then I'll feel better. My father is starting to worry about what's going to happen because he's getting older. He's forty years old and never had nothing, and now he's coming down to my place, my apartment, what I've worked for, and I'm only seventeen. I finally got my life situated, I'm stable, and it's something he never had and nothing he could ever give me. So I think it kinda bothers him that I got it on my own, and I didn't have to depend on him to give it to me. That might have an effect on him.

During all this time with TLP and Urban Peak, I was frustrated. I thought every day that things wouldn't work out. I thought I would just go ahead and do it by myself. That I could manage, and that they weren't ever going to help me get an apartment, anyway. They were just stringing me along. But it's harder than I thought. I'm kinda glad I got the help. But I'm the one that pushed myself to do it, because I wanted to, and I got here because of me. If I didn't do everything that I was doing, I wouldn't be where I am. They made a stepping stone, and I'm just kinda climbing all the way up.

I hope my experience shows that nothing's impossible. It helps if you have faith in what other people have done, or faith when people say that it can be done. It took me a long time, and it felt impossible, but I just never gave up. I was always trying to make something better, even if everything was getting worse. I just found something to plug away at, like my job, you know. The other thing is, you shouldn't depend on no guy, like I told you before, on making a quick dollar, turn a quick trick, and stuff like that. Just depend on yourself and find something that makes you happy. It is easier to just go out and find this man who will give you twenty bucks to do whatever with him. But then afterwards you feel like shit about yourself.

If you running away 'cause you think things are bad, have a plan or have some goals to accomplish. You know what I'm saying? You're leaving a certain place; you're going to another place to make things better. Just don't run away with no intentions. You gotta know what you want. Like when I left, I just wanted to get my life together, and with all the problems I had going on with my family, I felt it was the best thing I could do. And I kinda kept my job as my top priority, even though I was like living nowhere. I kept as my motive: Things will get better.

## How It Is with Friends from the Street Now

**Carrie has just asked a friend who dropped by, Gumby, not to come into her apartment with a beer.**

"No, can't drink here. Can't smoke here, either."

Since I got the apartment, it's kinda been telling me that some of these people don't ever want to move on. They'll just kinda live off of whoever they can. Once

they're out of one place, they're just gonna go somewhere else until it's warm enough to be outside. But they don't want to move on. They just wanna—I don't want to say "use" you, but that's how it is. You're cool with them, they're your friends, and they'll hook you up to smoke some weed or give you a forty. But some people are, like, real careless. They're just not ready to do nothing to help themselves, and it kind of makes me mad.

I want to help anybody who wants to help their self, because I know I needed all the help I could get. I wanna return that favor. But at the same time, if you're just gonna come in here and live up under me and not respect my wishes, then I don't think I should have to want to help you—I don't have to, that's basically it.

It's not as if I don't understand where they're coming from. I know I do. I'm just trying to not let people walk all over me. When I was in the streets, it was summertime, and in fall, it was cold at night, so I can imagine what it is like in the wintertime. Sometimes I feel like I should let everybody stay here. But if I don't agree with what they're doing, or I don't want to let them do it here in my place, and they're my friends, they should have respect for me, anyway.

One thing I know is that if you don't want to help yourself, then you should never complain about the situation you're in. I worked my whole time here except for my first, what, three weeks. I took advantage of things from people and places when they were offering help, and it was a benefit to me. But I don't think places like Urban Peak and TLP should help people that don't wanna do nothing. There are people up here in Denver that's been

◀ *At work (left)*

on the hill for three or four years, still in the same situation, and that takes away from giving more to another person that needs it or wants it more.

## Feelings about the Gun Now

**[I had made Carrie give me the gun until we could return it to the ex-cop whom she had bought it from. But when I left, she proceeded to get it back again.]** Ummmm . . . Well, I did give it back. I got really scared when things didn't go as good as I thought. I thought I would go home and just take care of all my business. I thought this was the time, that I could just take everybody off the face of the earth that I wanted to.

But my grandmother, she knew about the gun 'cause she was the first person that seen it. When she seen it, she thought I was crazy. I went to her house to shoot it off, and she was really scared for me. She's like, "That's not what you need to be doing." At the time, even my boyfriend was like, "Don't even think about it." He didn't let me go a lot to the city, because he didn't want me back in that stuff. And so, um, he kinda made me feel reassured, and I was like, "Okay, maybe I don't really need this, and I really don't need this in Denver." So I guess I got my little thrills off. I shot it, and I heard it 'n' stuff, and I just gave it away.

I'm kinda happy now I don't have it, although this very last time I went home for my grandma's funeral, I thought I'd get it back. But I didn't, and it's like, saved me. Sometimes I think in my situation I would be justified to shoot the men that raped me. But last time I was home, a couple of the main drug dealers in our neighborhood shot two of everybody's friends, associates, on my next corner—just took their heads off, and over stupid

stuff. Shot somebody in their own house, on their own corner. In their situation, I don't think it's justified. They don't care who you are. You say something wrong, they're gonna do it. My situation, I don't know. But every night since my grandmother's passed away, believe it or not, I pray to God that I'm glad I didn't do it. I actually pray that in the end they get their justice, and—it sounds crazy— but I pray for these people that done me wrong to make sure that somebody's looking out for them. If not, it's gonna get done to them. I guess I'm putting all my faith and all I have into God, and He's removed me from the situation.

Back in Denver, having the gun could have caused a lot of problems for me. When I went up to see my friend Buzz in the County [jail], it scared me a lot. I didn't like the treatment that I got, and I was just a visitor. He's been up there several times, but I know that when I think about myself, I wouldn't have it like this. I would be terrified, crying. I always think to myself now that if I ever want a gun bad enough, I'm gonna wait till I'm twenty-one. Then I can get it legal, and I will use it for protection. Then it doesn't cause as much chaos and confusion.

▲ *Carrie welcomes me to her apartment (above).*

## Last Thoughts

I'm constantly having difficulties, but I know that soon they're going to get better. Plus I'm like, "God, I can go to my apartment and just sit down and think about it. I can just sleep on it, and it'll get better, or it'll work out in its own way." Since I've been back from the funeral of my grandmother, my biggest difficulty was when I lost my job. It devastated me at first 'cause I didn't know what I was going to do. I didn't know how I was going to pay my rent. Everything else just piled up. But I was, like, well this is mine, I've worked for it, and you know something will work out. Hopefully I can figure something out in between. So I applied for other jobs and I got new ones—two of them. And it worked out better.

The work, it occupies me; it doesn't keep me at home. I don't like being alone. But I keep myself distant from enough people that I feel lonely a lot of the time. If

I'm constantly busy, then I'll be okay. The spare time I do have, I use to concentrate on getting my life more together, more stable, and that'll help me feel better about myself. I'm just trying to get myself where I want to be before I establish a bunch of friends. I don't want to be down at the bottom and have 'em keep me there. I want to be at the top, so when they try to pull me down, I'm already there. I'll know what I want, I'm headed strong, and they can't do it.

If you're trying, and you have someone constantly trying to pull you down, you might just fall. So I kinda keep a lot of older people in contact with me, 'cause they've got more wisdom. Even if they've never been in my situation, they kinda understand more, or they're more helpful or ready to listen than wanting to pull me down.

I don't know if I think I've done the greatest thing in my life. Other people might think, "Oh, God, I got into college—that's great!" Well, this has been my greatest thing, which I will cherish forever. That I finally made it to where I've always wanted to be. I finally made it here, and I hope a lot of other people can too, 'cause I've been in their situation, and I know.

Even now when I talk to TLP about them holding other people up from trying to get where I'm at, it makes me mad. Because, man, you don't do that to people when they're trying. You never put somebody down when they're trying, 'cause that's the worst thing you can do. People give up that way; they don't want to try no more 'cause no one wants to help them. So, but you know, eventually you'll get there. The only thing you can do is depend on yourself and be happy and say to yourself: This is my best move.

As you can see, I don't have much here, like material-wise. But that don't mean nothing to me, 'cause I'm still happy with what I do have, so thanks.

## JON SCHWARTZ / director of Urban Peak

Right now there's a push across the country to get back to family values. The runaway and homeless youth population gets neglected by that whole discussion in the sense of: what family? The majority of the kids we see have no kinfolk in that regard. If they do, they've given up any hope of being with them in the long haul. And yet no one wants to seriously look at why kids run, why there are problems in families. It's very, very damaging for a politician, regardless of what party, to bring that up, because the next thing you know, people are accusing you of not adhering to family values. The only thing you can say is that the responsibility to raise children lies with the parents—regardless of how many kids, long ago, lost all connection to their parents.

So, these kids on the street, they're on their own, and the term *family* really becomes a subjective one. They become family to each other. They adopt nicknames like "Mom" and say "That's my brother right there." All of this is their way of creating what they think everybody else has. They do succeed, in a way, and in my opinion, it's legitimate. They say, "This is my family," and they really mean it. And like the families they came from originally, their street families become dysfunctional in many ways. But they are families nonetheless.

Most of the kids who run away from home, who choose to leave home, have made a decision they've contemplated most of the time, for a very long time, and that's to leave. When they finally do it, they feel like they've taken all they can take. Lots of kids who tell you about when they first ran away will mention that they mentally said to themselves, "I'll give this one more try, and the next time Dad lays a hand on me, I'm outta here." Or, "The next time Mom is so stoned that she leaves the baby runnin' around in the street, I'm outta here." If their expectations get broken one more time, they're gone. So the process usually involves something directly to do with those people whose job it was to be their caretakers, and who've let the kids down. Then there are other cases where the mother or father is having the same kind of internal discussion: "Next time that kid of mine comes home late or drunk, or doesn't do what he's supposed to do, I'm kickin' his butt out." It's almost always a buildup.

But what you see, despite anybody's best intentions, is that the state really is this country's biggest dysfunctional family. Too many kids leak out of the system and wind up in places like this. You're dealing with long odds to begin with, because kids usually have been through so much by the time they get to be wards of the state. And then you're dealing with a system that really leaves a lot to be desired. It doesn't have the latitude and the creativity to figure out the right formula for each individual. Instead, it just drops them into a whole maze of interventions that aren't working.

As one big sort of organism, Urban Peak works, because we try to model a healthy parent in a lot of ways. We're the providers for the kids' basic needs; we're their limit-setters. They come here and see this big mass of people around them, and it all comes down to Mom and Dad and Brother and Sister. They don't know it, and they don't say it, but that's the way I feel. Because on the one hand, we give them what they need without asking, or without working for it, let's say. On the other hand, we remind them that ultimately no one owes them any favors; ultimately they're going to have to fly out there on their own. Good parents strike a balance between providing for and forcing autonomy in children. We do both of those things, and we have developed some talent for figuring out from kid to kid which combination is going to work best.

We'll even go, as parents will, to the extreme of not allowing kids in here if they're violent, or if they sit on their butts forever and ever, despite our prompts for them to do small things to get off the street. I think that's about the hardest thing we ever do here, but we've had kids come back a week later and say, "Okay, okay, I'll go ahead and do it." And that's the hope. If we overextend ourselves in terms of making life on the streets easy, then, like parents, we're not doing our jobs well. So that analogy of parenting is really applicable here. And I think these kids, the reason they all come here, without even knowing it, is because they're thirsting for it. So many kids don't understand their own ability, potential, joy, or their own beauty. They don't understand what they can do for themselves until someone tells them. That internal mechanism is really the biggest obstacle and always has been.

## ADAMS HOSKINS / caseworker at Urban Peak

You have to take seriously that these kids come from abusive homes because it's just reality. Nobody wants to be homeless. No kid wants to be on the street for a long period of time. Anybody who's not able to sympathize with that can go stand outside in the middle of winter in, let's say, Detroit, when the wind-chill factor is negative twenty. They can try to stay out there for five or ten minutes, and then they'll know that it's nowhere any human being would want to be. Just think about how a lot of these kids would stay outside and try to endure that rather than go home to deal with their parents. That's how bad it is at home.

These kids are our future, and to label them as "Generation X" is to label them as unknown or invisible. I think that's how many of the kids view themselves: as not being part of society. Society needs to grab these kids and let them know they are of value. Or else we're gonna have a lot of adults who are lost and who have been X-ed from the future.

The first issue you usually have to tackle is that of trust. I think a lot of these kids don't trust anyone. They certainly tend not to trust any adult, even or especially someone who's acting, in their eyes, in a caring way toward them. A lot of times these kids have run into adults who acted like they cared, but then later they realize that the adult they trusted now has them selling drugs, or stealing for them, or selling themselves. So it really takes quite a while in most cases to establish a relationship with these youth. The difference between me and the perpetrators who use the same tactics as I do, gaining

trust, is that they exploit the kids, where I try to help the kids get their lives together. Once you break that down, it's like a deep exhale, and you can move on from there and get back to the goals that you can set up together.

It can be very difficult at times to get a kid to become motivated and self-sufficient, because in many cases, they are very depressed and have no self-esteem. If you're homeless, and you're out in the street, you believe that you're no one. Most people who walk past you on the streets believe that, too. When someone keeps telling you, all your life, that you're no good, you begin to believe it. If something bad happened to you last night, then again the next day, and again, it stays hard-pressed in your mind. So you're less likely to do things. You're just sorta dragging around. For you and I, something else will come along that'll pick us up. But in the case of many of these kids, nothing comes along to pick them up. It's very difficult, because in the streets there are so many negative influences. Am I going to be able to pull you to the more positive side, or is everyone out there going to pull you to the negative side? It's a constant battle.

When the kids come in and start discussing their problems, I feel at that point I have their trust. But it's very frustrating, because I would like the whole world to give more focus to these youth and to realize their value. A lot of kids come in and out of this building each day who I know could be anything they wanted to be, if their talents were channeled in the right direction. But as long as they're shackled to the streets, that talent will just wither away and be wasted.

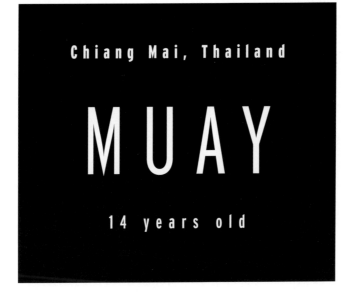

Chiang Mai, Thailand

# MUAY

14 years old

For the interviews, we sit in a small sunlit room in one of the homes of the NLC, and we can hear the animated voices of other young women enjoying their day. Muay was more comfortable telling me her story than I was hearing it. Her courage was a great help to me. After our talk, we ate an extraordinary lunch that the girls had prepared. Reverend Bethal acted as translator for the interviews.

Muay and I are with Reverend Lauren Bethal, the director of the New Life Center where Muay now lives. The New Life Center (NLC) opened in 1987, founded by two missionaries who recognized that many young tribal women in Thailand were being sold or tricked into prostitution. Getting girls out of prostitution can be very dangerous, so the NLC decided to focus first and foremost on prevention: identifying girls at risk; helping them to escape their precarious situations; and giving them access to a safe home, education, and vocational training.

For decades, brothels in Bangkok have been preying on the youth of the northern hill tribes, where literacy is low and few people speak the Thai language. Sometimes the traders even work in cooperation with village headmen. Although prostitution is illegal on the books, the institutionalized system of brothels continues to flourish without enough significant police intervention. The single greatest risk factor for native girls is having an opium- or heroin-addicted parent.

I'm Aka [one of the hill tribes of northern Thailand]. But I don't know exactly where I'm from. I come from many places. My father died when I was very young. My mother remarried, so I lived with her and my stepfather until I was six, when my mother also died. After that, my stepfather sent me to live with lots of other people, shifting me from one place to another. I would take care of children, do dishes, and various other things. My stepfather smoked opium.

▲ *A bed in a Bangkok brothel (above)*

have no real home. So
the Foundation for
Children kept me a year
in Bangkok, and eventually
I was able to come up
to the New Life Center.
I was about twelve.

## Coming to the New Life Center and Sharing with Other Girls

The people who brought
me here to the NLC
told me they were bringing me to a place where I would
be able to study and also would learn how to do handicrafts. When I got here, I realized that was very much the
case. I also feel there is a great deal of warmth that people
show to me here. When I was in the brothel, there were
times when I considered suicide. But I don't think about
that anymore. I know now there are people who want to
help me, who will take care of me, and who love me very
much.

With the other girls at the NLC, we all share experiences together, because people are interested. You know,
we've all had difficult lives, whether we've been sold or
not. When we're able to get it out, it helps all of us, and
it also helps others to have an understanding of what
we've been through. It helps me to share. . . . It's not
good for me to keep things inside. It's better to express
them.

## Being Sold

One day when I was ten years old, my stepfather sold
me to a woman who brought me down to Bangkok.
The woman took me to a brothel to be a prostitute. This
was very upsetting. I was very tiny then, so I told them I
was only eight years old. I lied so they wouldn't make me
work as a prostitute. A woman who worked there wanted
me to service the men anyway. Because I refused, they
beat me. The man who worked there finally agreed to not
make me be with the men because I was so small. But
later, I was beaten again. While I lived in the brothel, I
took care of the owner's children.

I thought about trying to run away, but I was followed wherever I went, so I couldn't. It was a very, very
frightening experience for me. I had been in the brothel
for three months when I was released with many other
girls by a police raid. The police interviewed everyone,
and I told them I didn't have anywhere to live, that I

## Things She Would Change
## If She Were a Village Leader

If I was the village headman—or shall we call it a "head person"? There are very few women that are head persons—I would ask for funds from the government to build schools in the villages so that all the children would have an opportunity to study. People don't get to study. Most of the women that I knew in the brothels, their education was very low. That's the problem. I think that if we just had the opportunity to go to school, then we would be a lot better off. And now with the problem of AIDS—it's likely that if everybody gets AIDS, then everybody is going to die. This is not something that is

necessary within society. And it shouldn't be that way. When I came to the NLC, I didn't even have any knowledge of AIDS or HIV.

Also, sometimes in the villages, the headmen are in cooperation with those who are selling girls, and it would be a good thing if they would at least put people in jail who were selling girls. They don't do that, you know.

## AIDS Education Weekend

I always wanted to be able to go to school, but I never had that opportunity. But now I can read and write, and I want to study as far as I possibly can. But what I really want to do is go back and help my people under-

stand what is going on. Especially young women—to help them not to have the same experiences that I had. That's why I took part in the AIDS education workshop, because I do feel it is my responsibility. Even though I don't really have a village of my own, I can go to other villages to teach about HIV and AIDS; to tell about women being sold and going down into prostitution; to explain why going to prostitutes, smoking opium, and injecting drugs can be such a dangerous lifestyle.

I believe the best way to teach people is for those who have had difficult lives or experiences, or who have been sold, to go back and explain these issues. We are the best ones to help prevent such things from happening to

others. Because if you haven't had these difficult experiences, then when you are talking to other people, they aren't necessarily going to believe you, to believe that these bad things really happen.

Before the training weekend, I was frightened about getting AIDS from people I was living with, because some of the girls at NLC are HIV positive. I didn't know if I would get AIDS from eating with people, from using the same bathrooms together, from living together. I didn't know whether I would get it by just living in a community. I learned that you don't get AIDS just by be-

▲ *Muay takes the floor (above).*

47

ing together. You can only become infected through un-protected sex, through blood, by sharing needles, or from mother to child. You don't get AIDS from eating to-gether or living together.

People who aren't HIV-infected are sometimes afraid to be with people who are, because they think AIDS is easy to catch. Without knowledge or information, there is no understanding. People become afraid and might tend to chase those who are infected out of their lives. Rather than this, what we need to do is to take care of infected people at home and to give them encouragement, support, and care. If we don't, they may become very dis-couraged and want to kill themselves. Infected people need not just sit around and think about the fact that they are HIV positive. They should be with friends who help give them a will and encouragement—friends who

tell them that they don't have to just think that they will die tomorrow or the next day, but that they need to keep up their spirits to live today.

After getting this in-formation from the train-ing, I feel like I'm being part of a solution to the HIV/AIDS problem. Youth should get more information about HIV/AIDS, and I would like to help. I want to teach youth that if they are going to have sex, they should use condoms, and even condoms are only ninety percent effective. I think that it is impor-tant for young people to teach other young people about HIV/AIDS. We have to, if we want to eliminate AIDS from our society.

## Muay's Faith

I want to go as far with my studies as I possibly can. And I also want to go to Bible school. I'd like to help other people know about God and God's love, because that's where my hope comes from. It's my faith. My favorite Bible verse is Hebrews 11:1—"Faith is being sure of what we hope for and being certain of what we don't see."

## REVEREND LAUREN BETHAL / director of the New Life Center

The majority of the girls at the New Life Center fall into what I would call the prevention category. Some of these girls were within days of being sold by their families into prostitution. Included in that group are young women who have shown leadership potential in their villages or churches but haven't had the chance for an education. Given the opportunity, they will go back and work even more effectively within the community. Our residents themselves are now our best recruits. They go back home at the term break; they talk to their friends and they talk to the people in charge, looking for young women who might be at risk.

The rest of our young women fall into the rehabilitation category, having formerly been part of the commercial sex industry in Thailand. They come to us from the lowest class of brothels—not from the tourist sex industry, where you have a lot more freedom and a lot more say over what you're doing, where maybe you're servicing only one person a night. The majority of our girls come from the real sleaze joints, where usually they were kept locked up. These girls come to us in a variety of ways.

It wasn't long after we opened the Center that family members started coming to Elaine and Paul Lewis, saying, "Would you help get our daughter [sister, cousin] out of a brothel? We thought she was going down to work as a housemaid, a dishwasher, whatever, and it turns out that, um . . . now that we've tried to follow up and find out where she is, she's not there, and we found out that she's having to work as a prostitute. So, can you help us get her out? We're helpless to do anything." Other nongovernmental organizations sometimes put us in

◀ *Reverend Lauren Bethal and Muay*

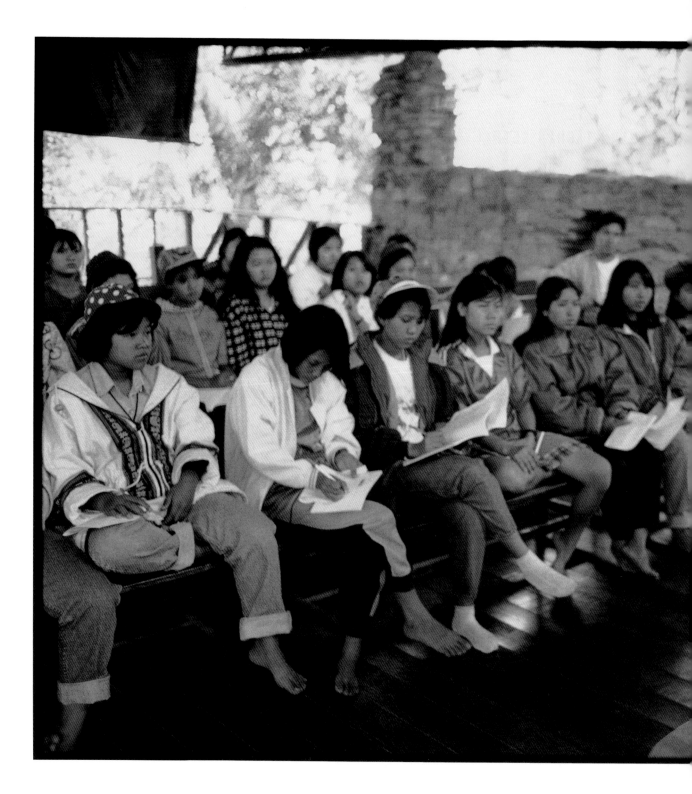

MUAY

touch with the Crime Suppression Division of the police. This particular subdivision was set up in order to help girls who were being held against their will or who are underage. Most of the ordinary policemen—I should say, many of the ordinary policemen—are involved in accepting bribes from the brothel owners and help keep the whole institution ongoing. Prostitution is illegal in Thailand, but it flourishes because of this type of assistance from the police. So we started helping to get girls out, and then after that, they would go to some other agencies in Bangkok and eventually be referred back to us if they were tribal.

For us, rehabilitation doesn't mean psychotherapists or counselors, because there aren't any trained in tribal languages. There are only eight Aka who have ever graduated from college. And I don't think you can do psychotherapy through a translator. Even if you were to try, the two cultures, Thai and Aka, are very, very different. So for us rehabilitation really means first of all providing a place that's secure, where the girls can trust the people with whom they're living. They know we're not trying to exploit them all over again. There aren't police coming in, and there aren't men running around.

Also, this is a very normal environment. Our girls live in homes, approximately thirty to forty girls in each house. The girls are in school at night. They all have the same goal of trying to get as much education as they possibly can, and they do handicrafts during the day. Learning handicraft skills can serve as a viable income if they return to their villages. We have an international market for our handicrafts.

◀ *Learning how to be an AIDS educator*

Quite honestly, I need somebody to come in sometime who can do a Ph.D. thesis on why we do not see aberrant behaviors with the girls. They've been tricked; they've been sold; they've been put in brothels, where they are locked up against their will; they were raped five, ten, twenty times a day. When they come to us, certainly at first, they're sometimes withdrawn—they're very distrusting of what's going on—but within several months, there's a healing process. You can just physically see it start to take place. And they end up leading very normal lives. They will get an education, get married, have children. They are very well-adjusted people. All without the kind of intervention techniques we feel are necessary in the West in order for that kind of transition to happen.

Among the hill tribes in northern Thailand, the Aka are going to be the most dramatically affected by AIDS. Traditionally they have multiple sexual partners before marriage. Many of the men have multiple wives, and there's quite a bit of sexual experimentation. Within a closed culture, this works fine; it's no problem. But when just one person introduces a sexually transmitted disease (STD), you're sunk.

*AIDS education weekend* ▶

Since the government has increasingly taken over Aka land for reforestation projects, the villagers can no longer grow their own rice and food. Many are forced to go down to the city to work. Families can't stay together, because Dad might be down in the city, working on a construction site, while Mom is back up in the village with the kids. Dad just follows the ways of his coworkers and goes to prostitutes. He then brings sexually transmitted diseases and HIV back to the village.

I quite honestly don't think a dialogue will change the cultural attitudes about prostitution. The fact that lots of people are dying of AIDS will make people realize that cultural behaviors must change. Seventy percent of the women who come into the New Life Center from

brothels are HIV positive. The girls who are HIV will talk to me about it. Some of them, I must say, still don't have a full comprehension of what it means. It takes a very long time for them to understand it. I ask them, "Would you like to talk with other people who are HIV positive or other people who might be able to counsel you?" They do not. They want it confined to them knowing, me knowing, and that's all. And I think that's very easy to understand, because in their villages, anyone who is HIV positive must leave. Their whole family will be banished from the village. The girls here who are HIV positive do not even know who else is also positive.

That's their secret, and we have to respect that confidentiality.

In an ideal world, I would like to form support groups. But there are no role models in Thailand for talking about HIV. No famous personalities in the country have come out and said, "I am HIV positive; let's talk about it." A few people have been encouraged to talk and have actually been paid salaries to do some talking about it, but they're not prominent. And they're very few and far between.

▲ *NLC young women in traditional Aka dress (above)*

I was very frustrated by the fact that I could not offer HIV/AIDS education in the tribal languages. There were no materials available, only Thai materials. If you go in and offer education to tribal people in Thai, they say, "Oh, it's not our problem, it's a Thai problem." So a friend of mine, who is a nurse, and I put our heads together and came up with a project, Health Education for Tribal People. Our teams target four languages in particular, with which our church already works closely. This church network is very strong and highly organized. Most

▲ *A school in an Aka village (above)*

of the material we develop is visual, because most of the people are nonliterate.

I decided that I really wanted my young women at the New Life Center to be trained as AIDS educators. Now when they go home for term breaks, they can go into the village and meet with any group, any informal group they can get together, even if it's only two or three friends. Women or men, if they're interested, fine, but I felt their natural target group would be their peers. So the girls go out, take our flip charts and posters, and start talking about AIDS education within the village itself. Forty-four of the women from the New Life Center have volunteered to come to this conference to be trained as AIDS educators. It'll be very different for many of the villagers to have someone come in and teach who is actually of the same culture and the same language group. And doing so can only enhance the girls' sense of self-esteem, since they'll know they are planting seeds of information, and the message they are bringing could make a huge difference in somebody's life.

I really feel that by giving the girls hope, providing opportunities for them to talk about their experiences, giving them skills for the future, helping them to understand that there are people who care for them—and helping them empower themselves by giving them an education, which is the core issue—we let them know they have worth and value. That they can stand up for their rights; that they don't have to be sold, tricked, or treated in other inappropriate ways. There is also a spiritual component to our work. We are a Christian organization; we don't make apologies about that. There's a real spiritual void that the young women are experiencing. Many times their whole societies, their tribal cultures are falling apart, and they come to us asking for spiritual nourishment. They want something to believe in; they want to believe in a higher being and in the love that the higher being has to offer. So they begin to realize that they are loved, they are accepted, they are cared for, by a higher being or by God.

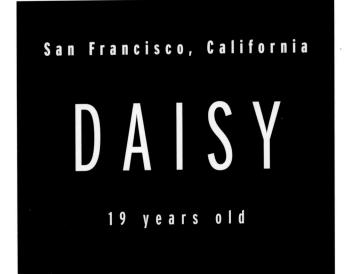

San Francisco, California

DAISY

19 years old

When I first met Daisy, I realized very quickly that he was one of the most alive people I probably would ever meet. What a joy! The first question Daisy asked me was, "Are you straight?" I replied, "Yes, is that a problem?" Laughing, he said, "We will see." It never was.

## Gay in Ohio

I remember sitting in class during the second week of school and listening to this teacher of mine, Mr. M., good old straight guy, captain of the freshman football team, and such an asshole. He was saying, "I hate faggots, fairies, and homos. Queer people are evil, and they don't deserve to walk on the face of this earth. I think it's funny that they all have AIDS." One day he was bitching about it, and I was just like, "You know, they're not hurting anybody." This was a big mistake on my part. My entire class was just, "Well, then you're a fag, because you stood up for someone who was queer."

Since I was never in the closet to myself about my sexuality, I had this ongoing fantasy that someday things would work out just fine, and I would be able to celebrate the fact that I'm queer. But I couldn't do it back then, because all I felt was ostracized. School got more and more hectic, and I just got more rebellious. I got really tired of all the shit every time I walked down the halls, with people calling me fag, queer, whatever. Then the violence began.

Every time I was in school, someone was slamming me into a locker or worse. I went to the bathroom between classes, and a bunch of hood boys decided that it would be real fun to beat up the fag. I ended up with a really bad bloody nose and a bad eye. I went into the office and told them, "I just got beat up. They were calling me faggot." In the office, they told me that if I wasn't so blatant, if I wasn't so extravagant and didn't draw attention to myself, this would never happen. I sat there going, "So I'm supposed to conform to these people's beliefs? Well, I'm not. No. I'm an individual. I'm allowed to express myself any way I want." And they told me, "Then you're going to have to deal with the repercussions." It was disgusting.

The amount of hatred that I incurred every day—I couldn't handle it anymore. So I started skipping school a lot. I would go to the three classes that I liked: creative writing, home ec, and mythology. I felt safe enough in those classes. I knew I wouldn't have my ass kicked. Then I would go home, because if I stayed at school, I would have to encounter certain people, or someone would send me a letter, or I would have to deal with teachers that were totally homophobic.

## Telling His Mother

When you grow up gay in middle America, you're constantly forced to hide. You're constantly forced to do pronoun reversal. When you say *she*, you mean *he*. When you say *he*, you mean *she*. Oh, I really like . . . *her*.

I was kind of forced out of the closet by my mother because she found poetry that I was writing about being queer. This poem called "The Same" was all about how I just wanted to walk with the "same" and love the "same" . . . sex, of course. My mother asked me a couple of times, "Are you gay?" I was like, "No. It's somebody else's poem. I don't want to talk about it." And she said, "If you choose to do . . . to have that life, then that's okay. I'll love you no matter what." I was just like, "I'm not gay."

That hurt, not to be true to myself. I was just really reluctant to tell her, but then later she found this really long love letter to this guy I knew. She and I were in the car, going to summer school, and she asked me again if I was gay. I said, "No, leave me alone." She asked me again, "Are you GAY? This is your . . . you wrote this. Are you gay?" And I was finally like, "Yes, goddammit," and then she was asking me, "How do you know?" " 'Cause I'm in love." And she's like, "Well, have you slept with him?" "No." "Well, have you slept with a man?" "Yeah." But she didn't want to hear about it. And then she asked me, "What about Heather?" And I was like, "Heather schmeather . . . Heather is just my friend, she was a cover-up." I used to pretend to have a girlfriend.

After talking to my mother, I just hopped out of the car and ran home. Later on, she came home early from work, because she knew I'd skipped school. She just told me that it was okay, and that she loved me no matter what, but I had to be really quiet about it because of my stepdad. He wouldn't be able to handle it. She was right, because three days later they got into a huge fight and their marriage was over. It wasn't just about me being queer, there were other things going on. But that was the end of that, which, believe me, wasn't a bad thing.

## Family Life

When my mom and stepfather got married, my mother was under that misconception of "I won't be able to survive on my own. Oh, my babies will need, you know, a male influence." So she got married. Before they got married, my sister and I thought he was great, but he went from being Mr. Good Guy to Mr. Monster. God, he was such an asshole. He just saw bucks when he looked at my mother and my grandparents.

This step-monster, the demon, adopted us, and as soon as everything was legal, he started beating us and fucking with us. He didn't really hit my sister physically, just fucked with her psychologically. He hated me. Once he really

hurt me, and I told him, "I'm gonna tell Mom. I'm going to tell what's going on." I remember him screaming at me, grabbing at me, and telling me that my mom didn't love me and that she told him that it was okay to hit me. That I could go ahead and tell her, and she would just get angry at me. I believed him, so I stopped talking to my mom about what was going on. It just got worse and worse, to the point where he just would lock me in my room.

At this time, I became really obsessed with animals. I had tons of critters: hamsters, frogs . . . but I had to hide my pets, because I wasn't supposed to have them. He would take them and flush them down the toilet. He would set a hamster free in the backyard, in front of me, and say, "It's gonna die." I would totally freak out.

Let me mention my real father. My dad split when I was three, and I've not seen him since. Supposedly he used to drive by the house and see us playing in the yard. I do have a desire to see him [sighs]. It's not even an issue of revenge, but he needs to be aware of some major issues, because he's got responsibilities. I don't care if he's forty-something. When you are part of the creation of life, you have obligations. You just don't deposit your seed and go skipping on your merry way. I'm not a salmon, you know.

I have only some vague memories of him, and most of them are pretty horrifying. I talked to my sister, and we both have the same memories of what he was like. My sister was my best friend and inspiration growing up. My biggest heartaches and my biggest traumas were with her. She was very protective of me. She had this certain way when I would get yelled at. She would pull me behind her and say, "Don't you hit my little brother." She was the only person I really had.

When we all lived with my grandparents, it was probably the only time in my childhood I was really happy. My grandparents are upper-middle-class Republicans who are very set in their ways. It's kind of scary. But they devoted a lot of time to me. My grandmother is an artist, which is really surprising, because she's very conservative and is into money. My grandfather was from a poor family. He earned his living working in a big steel mill.

▲ *Halloween (above)*

My grandfather's been the only real father that I've had, and the only real man that I've ever really loved. I was known as his little buddy, and I'm still called "Buddy." He would take his time to explain how to do this, that, and the other. He was trying to make me into a man. I always have memories of when my grandmother used to go to bridge club, because it was our special day. I'd follow him around, and we spent a lot of time together. I learned how to garden and build things out of wood. I remember sitting on my grandfather's lap, just bopping along, watching Mutual of Omaha's "Wild Kingdom," and "Grizzly Adams." He used to sit there and whittle ducks out of cedarwood. I was one of those kids who had frogs in his pockets and caught bugs and slugs and any critter that moved. My grandfather would always get me books on these bugs and other animals. I used to share a room with him when we lived with them, and he would tell me stories till I went to sleep, every night. He would just babble on and on about the war, or about when he was a boy. I really liked his stories. There was a point in time that I really loved him, and part of him was so magical. I have a really hard time with him now. It's really sad. . . . I mean, I'm able to be honest and say, you know, there's a difference between *like* and *love*. But I really care for him as my grandfather.

DAISY

My family has this habit of putting things in a bubble and pretending they don't exist. They do that with everything. Whether it's my sexuality, or the fact that I was getting beaten, or that I was a fourteen-year-old boy who never smiled. Whatever it was, they put it on the back burner or took me shopping, because that'll make me feel better. Here I am, part of a family that's part of Hamilton, Ohio's social elite, my parents both part of all these little organizations. It was just this bubble world. My family's very much like America.

## Sex Education

What I remember learning about HIV and AIDS is *not* learning about it. We were told about AIDS, but in Ohio there was no understanding or knowledge of it. In eighth grade, my friend Tiffany did a report on AIDS. It was still this homosexual disease on the big coast; it wasn't in Ohio. We were told there were twelve AIDS cases in Ohio in 1988–89, which is bullshit. There were a lot more, but only among gay men. My health teacher said you could tell if someone had AIDS because of the way they looked, so I thought I was safe. Total bullshit! My sophomore year, when I was in public high school, they talked about HIV/AIDS with all the other STDs, like chlamydia, gonorrhea, syphilis, herpes, hepatitis. Hey, I got to touch a condom, got to pass it around, was told to use it to prevent pregnancy, but was never shown how to use one correctly. I saw what a diaphragm looked like. And that was sex ed. All in forty minutes. Now I'm sorry. The high-school health curriculum sucks. There're probably still twelve people with AIDS in Ohio today.

I wasn't educated about the dynamics of homosexuality because it was seen as morally incorrect. I remember going to the library and looking up everything I could on homosexuals. The only thing I found was Harvey Fierstein's trilogy. That was it. The only time I got anything positive about homosexuality was from Father Brian, at my old private school. I remember asking in our sex-education class: What causes homosexuality? He couldn't answer that, but you know, he never said it was wrong, or that it was foul or dirty. He didn't say it was a curse from God, or morally incorrect, and that was really nice. But none of this really answered any of my questions. The only time I ever heard about people who were gay was when they got caught, you know, at a gay bar, or a backroom kind of thing. Or at some rest stop for picking up an undercover cop and getting arrested after having some kind of sex with the cop. Nothing positive, ever.

When I was fifteen, I went to this support group for gay men. A bunch of older men flocked to me because I was the new chicken, but then people wanted me out of the group because I was really young. The group was the only thing I had, but I wasn't getting much support. There was no place to turn when I needed to talk about all of this.

## Leaving Ohio for New York

I left Ohio because of all the homophobia, the hatred, and the bigotry that I encountered every day. The main reason for going to New York was to go to Harvey Milk High School. I couldn't take the idea of two or three more years of school, getting beaten up every day and being miserable. I presented this to my mother. I said, "Look, I'm moving to New York, and either I'm going to run away or you're going to let me go with your blessing. Either that or I'll end up being killed, or I'm going to kill

DAISY

myself. Those are your options." She then thought it was okay, you know, for me to move to New York.

My mother told me to attempt to contact the school and visit it and see what I thought. I knew enough people already there who could be support for me because I had met them at ACT UP demonstrations. I thought I could make it. Even if it meant selling my body, I had to get out of Ohio. Luckily I only had to do that once, and it wasn't really like selling my body. It was just sleeping with somebody for a place to stay. But it wasn't too bad, 'cause I had fun. I attempted to prostitute myself one time, but I guess I was just too fat and ugly [laughing]. No one wanted me. A blessing in disguise.

I was homeless the majority of the time. I just crashed with all these different people, who were all very accepting and generous and who did a lot for me.

## Sex Doesn't Equal Love

I started my sex life by having unprotected sex. One reason was because I wasn't really educated by anyone, but it was also because I wanted someone to love me. I could try going to a pharmacy and deal with the scariness of being fifteen and getting condoms, or going to gas stations and getting them from a vending machine. Mainly I had to rely on the men that I slept with to have condoms, and if they didn't have one, I ran the risk of them kicking me out if I said no. At the same time, my hormones were kicking in, and I wanted to sleep with them if they found me attractive.

Mostly it was just obnoxious. I was really scared about saying no. I was very naive and trusting. I always thought that sex equaled love—that if someone said you're sexually attractive, and you slept with them, then immediately they would really love you and fall in love with your soul. They would get what they wanted, and I would get what I wanted. That's what I thought love was all about. But love, I think, is something that doesn't come from a one-night stand. It's about meeting your soul mate. It's finding that person who is an individual and is just right for you, for whatever reason, and then growing from them and from yourself.

You can have sex with someone if it's just for sex; that's fine and dandy. Sex is a really healthy thing, and being sexual creatures, we should be allowed to explore sexuality and sensuality as long as we are responsible. Being responsible for our own actions is the key. But sex doesn't equal love, although it's a part of love. Unfortunately it took me a long time to figure that out, and it was a little bit too late. But at least now I know it, and maybe other people can learn from my fuckups.

## Finding Out That He Is HIV Positive

Before I moved to New York, I knew that some big shit was going on with my body. I'm very psychic with my body, and something was telling me I had HIV, but I was just really scared to deal with it. When I was between the ages of eleven and fifteen, I never wore a condom or had a partner wear a condom, and I was really having a lot of sex. I got tested in Ohio, before I moved, and they said that it was negative. I was sixteen then, but I've been HIV positive for, I'm assuming, four years, and I have not had unsafe sex since that test. I refuse to believe that I got infected while having safe sex, and anyway, I only had sex three times during the two years I was in NYC, and it was always safe. The only thing I can think of is that maybe I had just gotten infected before I was tested. You do have that window period.

I had moved to San Francisco by the time I was eighteen. Some people there approached me on the street to take this young men's survey, "We need young gay men," and it included blood work, etc. And I said: I should take an HIV test, and this survey is important. They'll get a perspective of someone who knows their stuff and is practicing safe sex. So I took the test a day or so before I turned nineteen on February twenty-sixth, and I was told I had to wait a week for the results.

On my birthday, I ran around the city doing this and that, getting ready for the party I was having. I was so, so happy to be alive. I was just overjoyed. I was on Market Street, in front of the store where I was working, and I just screamed "I LOVE LIFE!" I was so happy it was my birthday. I felt wonderful. It was the best birthday I've had thus far, other than having to go home and clean my room for the party, which kind of sucked.

The day before I went to get the test results, I went to a workshop where I was learning a new method of meditation and inner growth. The next day, March first, I remember getting on the train and just saying, you know, "Brace yourself, brace yourself," basically because I knew something was up. I was expecting the worst, but at the same time I wasn't. It was like, if I say I'm going to have it, then I won't have it. I went in, and there's this really cute, cool boy Danny, who did all the blood work. We were just chatting, and he was really patient with me, but I knew that shit was up. Finally I'm like, "Hello, give me the news," because I know what you're going to tell me, anyway.

And he says, "You're HIV positive."

And I was just like, "What?"

"You're HIV positive." I . . . I just went numb. Just so shocked. I didn't know what to say. I saw that it was my blood that had been processed, and that they had given me the PCR, which is the totally complete HIV test. I was definitely positive, and so numb. I remember him holding my hand, and I didn't cry. I just sat there, not wanting to believe. I was in denial, but at the same time I wasn't. I just had to leave. I had to go and walk around. I knew I was positive, I could feel that I was positive, but I just wouldn't face it, you know. Walking down Market Street, I was so . . . angry at life. It just wasn't fair. I had done so much work in the field of HIV/AIDS activism. I had done so much with people; trying to prevent HIV in other people's lives, helping people to participate in things to increase their awareness, having people tell me, "You really helped me; you probably saved my life." How could I be positive? It didn't make sense.

I was just a mess, so I went home because I couldn't find anyone to talk to. At home, I just rocked on my bed back and forth, back and forth, back and forth. Like when people go insane. I called my mom and told her to sit down, and she was like, "Oh, shit, what now?" I told her and she started bawling, and then her friend got on the phone and was so rude to me. She asked, "What did you do?" And I said, "I'm HIV positive." And she asked, "How did that happen?" And I was just like, "Through sex!"

I wasn't able to deal with it, and I almost let down and cried. I started to cry a little bit, because my mom was crying. But then I took this entire mothering role, which I always do, had to nurture her, had to soothe her and tell her that it was going to be okay and all that jazz. My mother was a mess. I had my friends Jacqueline and Alex come over, and they got me really stoned. I just kept trying to make light of it and laugh at it. Then I just sat

on my bed; I didn't know what to do. Jacqueline didn't know what to say. I was just so freaked out, and finally later that night I just crashed.

On that day, so much of me died. I couldn't be carefree, I couldn't be wacky and zany anymore. I got to experience what it's like to be an eighteen-year-old, but ever since I've been nineteen, I've been positive. I no longer will be able to be a young person. I've got to be so conscientious about everything, I've got to be so careful about where I go and things that I do. My body is so susceptible to infections because of my weakened immune system. I just had to grow up so much. I look back at who I was a year ago at this time, and the change is so drastic, you know, how responsible and adult I am. I can't be a kid.

It's really hard for me to have this pretty dream of having my house, in the middle of nowhere, planting a tree, and watching it grow. I can't really . . . it won't happen. I want to have a baby, I want to raise a baby, but I can't. I can't do that to a child—to consciously say, okay, I'm going to be your dad, but I'm probably going to die soon, so you've got to deal with it. It's such a reality that I'm going to die of this. I mean, I enjoy life, and it's not like I'm going to lock myself inside my room and, you know, "Well, I'm going to die anyway." But I don't have much time.

It's not that I'm not going to try. I have to try; you've gotta fight.

## Getting Support

I went to Cole Street Clinic the day after I found out I was positive. I was told to go there to figure things out, and that's where I met William. I was really, really freaked. We looked at the results, and I remember him

saying, "What are you going to do?" And I was like, "Well, I've got to change everything; I've got to quit biting my nails because that will get me sick, and I've got to do this and that, and I've got to change this and I've got to change that." I was like, change, change, change, change. He asked, "No, what are you going to do today?" And I was like, "I'm going to go skating." William just said, "Good, go skating. Get on your skates, go . . . and have a good time, go . . . enjoy yourself."

William really helped me. In general, William was probably the best gift I got when I found out that I was positive. His nurturing, the fact that he honestly, bona fide cared and liked me. He gave me his time and energy. There's so much safety I feel from William. Even though I thought I could totally deal with it—I mean, I've had friends come to me who are HIV positive, and I'd comfort them—it's not the same. When it's your case, I mean.

If William hadn't told me to go skate, I probably would have been a little neurotic mess. A few days later, I finally came down a bit from the shock. I started to cry. First I started to moan, then I started to wail, and then I was just shaking. I was crying so hard that I almost had convulsions. I fell over and was on the ground crying and was just a mess. You know, I'll never forget that day. . . . I've never cried so hard in my life.

I was living with these straight people, and they didn't know what to do about it. I was one of the first gay people they'd ever lived with—you know, one of the token gay friends [laughing], but they'd never known anyone with HIV. One of them was going to move out, and then she was, you know, "fuck that." She realized that she didn't need to move. It was a very spooky time, and they were all very supportive. But I realized I couldn't live with them, that I needed to be in a safer environment where I was with people that I could trust and who knew what was going on with the disease.

When I found out I was positive, I was so lucky to be in San Francisco because there was something available like Bay Positives. I was able to be with other young people, close to my age, who were going through the same sort of crisis and situations that I was going through, at different levels—young people who have been dealing with HIV for four years saying, "Hey, this is my experience." It gave me the space to talk about issues that other people could identify with. If I had gone to a regular group, like the majority of HIV support groups which are all for older men, it would've been a different level of consciousness. I'm in a different phase of my life compared to them. They're all into their careers, and here I'm not even in college yet. So I needed to have a group where I could feel safe and be comfortable dealing with my disease, and I made some really good friends.

Cole Street Clinic is phenomenal, because it's specifically for young people and they have youth advocates. People will go with you to different appointments, covering the whole spectrum of youth services, not just HIV. It's very youth-friendly and nonjudgmental, and everyone speaks the language. It's not just clinical. They offer a place to hang out, to watch TV, to sleep if you have to, to get a snack in your stomach, to talk with someone about your issues, plus covering medical needs. They offer Western medicine and holistic medicine, like acupuncture and Chinese herbs. That in itself is incredible, that young people are getting this for free, because it costs a buttload.

I'd be fucked without Cole Street. I don't know where I would be. I'm sure I would be having to go to the local hospital, waiting in line for eight hours just to get someone to look at me, who wouldn't know me, who wouldn't really care about me, and every time I would see someone different. I don't think I would feel safe at all. I'd be in a really bad space because of not being able to find any sort of health-care coverage. Most young people aren't insured, unless they're insured by their parents, and eventually they lose it. Goodness knows I lost my insurance on my birthday this year. Happy Birthday, Daisy—and oh, by the way, you're HIV positive.

## How Daisy's Mission Began

My mission is to educate young people about HIV—to show those who are positive that it's okay to be positive; that it's not just a death sentence. To show them that they can have a very full and exciting life, and that they can love themselves, empower themselves, and not let society destroy them with all the stigma and dogma.

When I'm speaking, I've had young people come up and tell me that they're positive. I'll be the first person they ever talk to about it. The only other person who may know is the person who told them the results. They can't tell their friends, they can't tell their families, they can't tell anybody. They're stuck with this information, and they don't have any light of hope. All they see on television is the dying corpse. They see the AIDS victim; they see the AIDS patient, lying in bed all shriveled up, covered with tubes and hoses. You have Magic Johnson, who I think was on the right track of helping young people and really bringing the message out, but he's so homophobic. It's not good for him to sit there and say,

"I'm not gay. Hell, no." So it becomes okay for him to have HIV, and for everybody else, it's morally wrong.

Then Ryan White was tokenized as the innocent victim. Those nasty old faggots—they're the ones. If they hadn't given blood, Ryan wouldn't have this. Ryan White was a fighter, and I give him a lot of credit, and I think he's a fabulous human being. But I get angry at how he was portrayed in the media. He was made special, but actually everyone who has this disease should be treated equally. They need to show that it's a human disease—Human Immunodeficiency Virus. The key word here is HUMAN. We are people before we have the disease, and we are people after we have tested positive.

What's needed is compassion, respect, love, and nurturing. It's a good thing that these young people are able to identify with me, and that I'm helping to break through their walls. They feel that they can trust me because I've been trusting of them.

I want the people who are negative to stay that way. I want to show them that they don't want this disease, and that they always need to be safe. They need to empower themselves and make proper responsible choices—sex choices, love choices—to keep themselves alive and healthy. AIDS and HIV are not the only things that are out there that will destroy someone's life. There are so many things that loom in the darkness. I want to put a face to this disease because for so long, fifteen years or so, there's been none. I'm the second generation of AIDS, and it's really scary that there's going to be even more. I don't want there to be a third generation. It needs to stop. It needs to end. I want people to wake up. I want young people to see that I'm a real person and not some skinny little corpse.

I actually started my mission a long time ago, when I got involved with ACT UP in New York. A friend of mine was living with AIDS. I don't know if he's around anymore, because I've lost contact with him, which is really sad. But Jim was really, really sick. He was part of the DDI access trial, and I remember him sitting on this portable potty all day long, shitting out clear liquid. He was just one big tube. His insurance was running out, so he couldn't stay in hospitals and had to be at home. He couldn't afford a nurse, and he needed someone to help him; I needed a place to stay, so I helped him. I had to reconnect his electrolyte drip, so he wouldn't totally dehydrate and die. Help him up, take the bedpan and clean it out, and just help him by putting Preparation-H on his bedpan sores. It was so embarrassing for him to have some young person help him in that way and be able to pick him up because he was so thin. It made me so angry, but it made me wake up.

My friends Sophie and Max, who I went to school with at Harvey Milk, both were sixteen or seventeen and positive. That was really scary. They were young people. Supposedly Sophie's still alive, but no one's talked to Max, so I don't even know. My classmate, my high-school classmate, could very well be dead. At the time, it

▲ *Speaking about HIV and AIDS at a local high school (above)*

DAISY

made me get out there and scream and yell, and find the power of activism. My activism got stronger and stronger until the death tolls just got so high in New York that I had to quit for a while. I could not take it anymore. Here I was, screaming and yelling and doing interviews about sexuality and HIV prevention, as a young person who supposedly wasn't infected.

When I first found I was positive, I couldn't get back involved right away. I had to separate myself from this disease. But finally I realized one day that I had to get back into it, because it was what I did well and it was really important. I had to put myself on the line, if that's what it took. I can't expect anyone to represent me other than me. I have to do it myself.

## Acceptance

For me, the difference between *queer* and *gay* is the generation gap. A lot of older gays and lesbians fought for the right to be called gay. *Queer* is odd, eccentric, nonconforming—a lot of these connotations are really positive. And being queer also means being very accepting, of other people and their sexuality and their gender; *queer* takes in everything. You can even be straight and be queer at the same time. I have a male body, but I don't really see myself as having a male mind. I'm just myself. Part of the thing about my name, Daisy, is being part of a chain; there's a very spiritual element to my personality.

I've had a lot of enlightenment from being HIV positive. It was probably the strongest life change of all. HIV has changed me for the better in many aspects. I'm not as petty as I was before; it made me love myself a lot more; it made me face up to myself; and it made me face up to the fact that the sexual part of me is really important. I see that life is precious. There's so much more to it than what so many people see. It's about enjoying each day—enjoying, you know, winter, or oooh . . . it's fall. Look at the trees; I mean really look and see them. I try to find fun and pleasure out of at least something every day. It's all really important, because there is no cure, and that's something I'm very aware of too, you know: I'm gonna die. Probably within the next five years.

I get really angry when people say, "You're so young," because, yeah, I am young, but the scary fucking thing is I'm never going to be old enough to say "I remember this place." I want to scream and say, "I'll probably never see thirty." I just don't see there ever being a cure. People can say you've got all the time in the world, and I'm like, no, I don't. I don't see myself . . . well, I've gotta make the year 2000, which is a good six years away, and that would make me ten, eleven years living with HIV/AIDS. Everybody's thinking the average life expectancy with HIV/AIDS is seven years, so supposedly I only have two more years to go. Yee, ha . . . but I don't believe that. I won't let myself believe that. I've got too much work to do.

I get really envious of my friends when they talk about their long-term goals, and I can't plan more than a month ahead. I don't know what I'm going to feel like, or where I'm going to be, or what I'm going to be able to do. I can't plan that far ahead.

I feel very important. But most important, I'm important to me. I'm selfish in many aspects. I mean, the only person in this world that I need to look out for is myself, and if in helping other people I can look out for myself, then I will. I feel my message is important and that my voice is important. I love myself a lot. I don't think I'd be around if I didn't. Sometimes I get really frustrated with my life, but I'm not really frustrated at myself. I'm frustrated at the law of things that just kind of work against me, and all the new trials and tribulations. "Here you go. Here's something new for you to struggle over." But so far, I've made it through everything.

I just hope that I affect people in many ways and help young people see in some way that life is really precious. I want to tell them: Don't worry about what people think of you. Worry about what you think of yourself. You're the biggest judge of all. Life is about enduring, but it's also about enjoying yourself, being who you are, and accepting who you are.

## WILLIAM ROGERS / counselor

I think there is total denial about adolescents having sex. People aren't talking about it, but it's clear that adolescents are having sex and are becoming infected with HIV. One-quarter of the AIDS cases are people between twenty and twenty-nine years old, and if there's a common incubation period of ten to fifteen years, then most of these people were probably infected during their adolescent and teenage years.

What people don't want to admit is the fact that young people are sexual and therefore are at risk for this

disease. Instead of talking about adolescent sexuality, people say, "Well, let's tell them to abstain." Well, guess what, babe? They're not abstaining.

The unfortunate piece of this is that so many young people are going to die before all the layers of denial are uncovered. At some point, the world is going to get it. But at that point it's going to be too late. We're going to lose so many people who had so much potential to give. So do we stick with some ridiculous moral philosophy about "just say NO to sex," or do we say, this is how you can have sex responsibly? If you want to abstain, fine. If you wanna have sex, fine. It's your choice. You need to decide when you're ready, and then

we'll be ready to teach you how to have sex responsibly.

Starting prevention education earlier could be, for example, letting little kids just play with condoms. It's nothing to be ashamed of. Not like, "This is a condom. Oh my God." But like, "This is a condom, and this is what I use to protect myself." Get kids familiar just with the idea of condoms. Then you can have open, frank discussions in peer-led groups, because peers will talk to peers before they'll talk to adults about a lot of this.

You can discuss what to do in situations when you're with somebody that you really want, and you can dis-

▲ *Daisy and William (above)*

cuss how you feel. You feel like you're a better person, a worthwhile person, and an attractive person because this person wants to sleep with you. "Well, I must be a good person because this person wants to sleep with me." Now that's a very powerful emotional dynamic. So how do you then say, "But if you're not willing to use a condom, then I'm not willing to sleep with you"? There can be a really intense pull not to use a condom. How do we deal with that? Let's talk about it.

Young people also need to have a forum to be able to discuss things when they slip up. "Yeah, I didn't use a condom the last time I had sex, and this is why." To have their peers be able to say, "Yeah, I know. That happened to me two months ago, and I don't know why I didn't use a condom."

I think the underlying issues around self-esteem have to be dealt with, because low self-esteem often translates into having unsafe sex. In addition to saying, "It's really important that you use a condom," we need to tell young people that as individuals and as a whole group, they are important. "You are worth it, and if there's something that you don't want to do in a sexual situation, don't do it."

In terms of the young person who's HIV positive or living with AIDS, we need youth-friendly services, and we need health facilities that are accessible by public transportation. We need to give young people the tools to advocate for themselves, to question the services they are being given, and to learn how to manage very complex health-care systems and insurance. We need to help young people learn how to negotiate safer sex even after they test positive. We need to educate about nutrition, about drug use. If someone was getting high and having sex before, they're going to have similar issues now. We have to help the young person understand that they can accomplish some of their goals—maybe many goals, maybe all of them.

Instead, young people with HIV are told, "You are gonna die. You have a shortened life expectancy." If you had low self-esteem before testing positive, and then you were told you have shortened life expectancy, what do you think your self-esteem is now? There is also the issue of people with HIV being blamed for their status. It's like, "Oh, it's your fault." Then you have young people living with HIV who are part of a community of young people who are also getting sick, and are dying, and somehow they have to carry on with their own lives, knowing that it's the same disease and that at some point they will probably succumb to a similar death.

So here are all these things piled on top of this already low self-esteem. To start to help young people achieve their goals, part of what has to happen is to help them understand that who they are and what they are doing right now is enough. I don't care if you're not working—whatever you're doing, I don't care—just being alive, and in the world, and taking care of yourself is enough. You don't have to be anything more than that. We need to say: "Know what? You're a great person."

M A R K   P A U L

" D A I S Y "

Born:
*February 26, 1974, in Hamilton, Ohio*

Died:
*January 7, 1996, in San Francisco, California*

# RANSON

14 years old

**WAKAN TANKA:** Great Spirit; the Creator. He is the greatest of all the spirits ever created.

**TUNKASHILA:** Grandfather. The oldest entity and the highest relationship in Heaven and Earth. *Tunkashila* is interchangeable with *Wakan Tanka* in prayers.

**WANBLI WIYAKA:** The Eagle Feather. There is honor in the possession of an eagle feather. Owning a feather is owning part of *Wakan Tanka*, who transmits prayers to greater heights by being present in the eagle.

**INIPI:** Sweat lodge. Lakota nations use the *Inipi* to purify themselves in body, mind, heart, and spirit, so they may better speak to their Creator. The *Inipi* is used for a vision quest or sun dance.

**TIWAHE:** Family

**TIYOSPAYE:** What holds the family together. The larger the extended family, the stronger it is. *Tiyospaye* means good character and cohesiveness in the family structure.

**INA MAKA:** Mother Earth. *Ina Maka* originated from *Inyan* ("rock") in the beginning, and so she is very sacred. She is Mother to all things that grow on earth.

**CANKU LUTA:** The Red Road; the "path with heart." All good people try to walk this road. When they fall off, they must rise up and get back on it. The Red Road runs north to south on Mother Earth. After death, a departed spirit goes south to get on the spiritual path and must travel the road to reach the kingdom of *Tunkashila*.

**Ranson, with the help of the mentoring program at his school, is trying to continue on with these beliefs, customs, and ideas. The Ateyapi Society mentors are Native American men and women who come to the Rapid City schools to help Native American youth succeed in gaining an education and to help them connect with their cultural heritage.**

## Family

I was born and raised in Rapid City. Just turned fourteen on March third. I think when I was born, I was living with my mom and dad, but I don't remember. Mostly it was my great-grandmother, Katherine, who I've been living with and who's been raising me and my sister. My parents were usually out doing bad things, drinking and stuff like that. Off and on, they would pay attention, but not as much as a parent should. My mom paid more attention, but now she's in a state penitentiary for using and selling drugs. She calls once or twice a week. She was sentenced to three years, I think. She might be able to get out on good behavior and be on probation this summer. We get along good.

I don't know where my father is. When my father was around, and when he was sober, we would have a good time. He'd always talk about art—the art he does with rocks and stuff like that. His carvings are beautiful. He talked about how he was going to teach me, but he never did.

They wouldn't do the drugs and drinking in front of us or nothing, but we'd know. They'd always have friends come over, and they'd all go into the back room and do

what they were doing. You could hear 'em doing it, if you got up to the door and listened. Sometimes me and my sister would put our ears to the door, just out of curiosity at that age, you know. With my mom and dad, it does disappoint me that they had to get involved with that kinda stuff. Why couldn't they just have been around me more, do more things with me, just be more of a parent? You knew in your heart that they really wanted to quit, that they really wanted to be with you, and they wanted to do the best a parent could do. But it's just so hard for 'em to quit. I feel sorry for what they've

▲ *At home with Grandma Katherine (above)*

done, and I feel sorry for them doing it. But I'm just used to it.

My great-grandmother Katherine, she's always there. You could say she's my mom and dad. Every night she says, "I love you—sweet dreams" three times, to be sure I got it. And in the morning she pushes me. I hate waking up, but she's right there, "Get out of bed." I go to her for real personal problems. She's just a problem solver. And even when I got in trouble 'cause I took a knife to school, she tried to support me. You know, she said, "I can't believe you did this; you're a bonehead." But I knew she still loved me, and I think sometimes she kids about what her real feelings are to keep me from feeling bad.

**▲** *A local antidrug rally (above)*

## Ranson's Experiments with Drugs and Alcohol

I've drank some beers a couple of times, once or twice. I never could understand how someone could like beer. I just tasted it and thought I was going to puke. I smoked pot. Well, you know, my friends, they'd maybe get a joint or something and say, "Hey, I've got some pot. Let's go smoke this somewhere." So I went, like, to not be the nerd or something. Peer pressure. Peer pressure is big: wanna belong. You follow your friends. That's how you get into that stuff. 'Cause I probably wouldn't have cared, but it was with my friends, so I'd go and smoke it with them. But I never . . . I faked like I inhaled. I was scared.

So then you start separating who your friends are. But if you're really close with your friends, you know, you don't want to push 'em aside; you want to help them out. You say, "Hey, what are you doing? You don't need this." It's been a while since I used anything. I consider myself clean.

I want to know so much. You have to be clean to learn, to be a leader. If you drink, it's going to mess up your mind, and then you just can't do nothing right anymore. This morning I woke up, and a friend of the family had spent the night. She came in kinda late and she was drunk. She couldn't drive, so she had a friend drive her over. This morning she woke up, and you could tell she was still buzzed. She was just walking into walls. How are you going to be a leader if you walk into a wall, running into people and stuff? It just don't work. I'm around drugs and alcohol a lot. It's a problem in Rapid, and I think it's getting to be a bigger problem than it used to be. But it really doesn't bother me no more. It used to bother me, but mostly it's just an everyday thing now; you adapt to it. I do. The more I learn about myself, the less I want to use it.

A lot of my friends, they're using. I've seen a lot of families hurt bad by drugs and alcohol. In the homes, there's lots of child abuse. Kids alone all the time, parents never there. Kids living with their grandparents so they can eat. Seeing their parents walk around drunk, maybe their father beating their mom. It's not something my

friends usually discuss, but it's there. If you don't want it to be there, you just try not to care about it and just try to totally erase it from your mind. So when you're with your friends, you want to play and have fun. But I know it would help if some of them had someone to talk to if they wanted.

## The Mentoring Program

I got called to the office once 'cause I guess they were looking at my grades or something. They told me about the mentor program, kind of laying down the basics. "We think you need help, and we want to help you." This mentor would come to all my classes, and I don't

know why, but I just didn't like the thought of having a tutor. I didn't want to be teased, I guess. Having a tutor sounded like a production.

I did feel more comfortable when I learned that my mentor was going to be Sydney. I dated her daughter a while back, so I was kinda used to seeing her. It was a good feeling that it wasn't a stranger.

In some ways I thought I needed the help, because it's hard for me to do my work. I just never did like it. I'm lazy, I guess you could say, with work. I don't pay attention. Really I didn't want it because I knew that if I just did it myself—paid attention, did it, handed it in—the work would be easy. Because, you know, I could

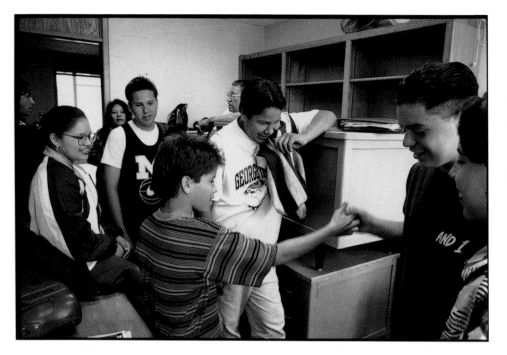

ness. Me, I would like to be in the NBA or NFL. I'm pretty stable on that dream. I know I need a lot more practice in sports, but you also have to have an education 'n' stuff, in case you don't make it. Then you'll have something to fall back on. Since I've been doing better in school, I guess you could say that I feel better about my self-esteem. It's raised

do it when I wanted to. I needed kinda like a push.

When I first started the mentor program, I maybe was just barely passing. Then my grades improved, and pretty much my grades went from Fs to Bs. I just think about how it was before Sydney was helping me, and I think about how it is now and how much of a change it's been. School was boring: I'd sit in school and someone would talk. You'd never get your work done. Sit all day, from eight to three—now, that's boring. But when you do start working, it's not as boring. I'm not saying that working is all fun, but it's better than just sitting around. That's something I notice a lot.

I know you can't go in pursuit of your dreams without working. I know that I have talent, and I'm not shy. I'm not afraid to go for my own individual goals. Some people might want to be lawyers or doctors, maybe not even that. Maybe they just want to have their own busi-

▲ *At school (above)  /  Making tobacco ties (far right)* ▶

my personal confidence. Sydney, she really tried to impress upon me that it was important to work on my education. I know it's important for me to take part in this program 'cause it helps me out in most everything.

A lot of other kids could be helped, but some are just scared. Scared of what they don't know. Some kids think having a mentor is like having a tutor, and having a tutor is the same as being dumb. It's something you can get teased about, and they're scared of what might happen to their reputation.

I've got a friend who's already in the program, but it's not helping him, because he's not listening to what the mentors have to say. He doesn't wanna hear, doesn't wanna listen, and he thinks he's more right than they are. He just doesn't care. He's involved with the drugs and stuff, and he don't want to quit it. It's peer pressure from the gang relations he hangs around with, and I don't know if his parents are there or not. He just does it for attention, and he wants someone to care about him. But

then he's afraid of having someone who could care about him, like a mentor. Even if someone does try, I don't think it's gonna help, 'cause he's going to push it away. He's really confused. But you just gotta not be scared. There's nothing wrong with saying, "I'd like some help."

I also think they should add on more female mentors and start letting girls into the program. 'Cause there are females out there who don't know much about their culture. They should be able to learn like we do.

## Cultural Identity

I first became interested in Lakota culture because of my dad, even before I knew Sydney and Dave [Sydney's husband]. My dad was kinda cultural. He would have the feathers and artwork in the house. I really wanted to learn more about it, the language and how to speak it. Then I met Sydney and Dave and figured, now's my chance, and I wanted to take advantage of it. Sydney, she kinda laid it on me first. She asked me if I wanted to go to a sweat this one weekend. And I thought, yeah, I wanna do this, go to a sweat, go on weekend camping trips, get more involved with all of it.

As we went through it, I started asking more questions about everything. She might say an Indian word or something, and I'd ask: What was that now? What does this and that mean? The language. The circles, and how there's a flow to everything. The tobacco ties I've just learned how to make, the eagle feather, and other things like that. Sydney and Dave are a big help in that. I'm still having trouble understanding it; I'm just beginning to learn it. But it's important for me to learn more 'cause, you know, maybe there's a place in your heart for it, and it's just empty right there, and you want it to be filled.

It's a good feeling to know the culture is still there. You go off there to do sweats and tobacco ties, and just walking around, you can feel the spirituality out there. You can imagine how it was hundreds of years ago, wearing the moccasins and the leather and doing everything from scratch—skinning buffalo and using every little bit of it. If you don't learn all of this, how are you going to stand up for it? I'm standing up for this, because I want to, but I don't know enough about it yet. You gotta know what you're doing. You just can't go out there and back up what everyone's saying without knowing about it. But when you do know about it, it helps your confidence. It just helps everything.

You can go higher, you know, by not being embarrassed to tell people who you are. I am me. I'm not scared to be an American Indian. I guess you could explain it like that. It's sad that in Rapid or on the reservations, so many Lakota people don't have any culture, beliefs, knowledge. It makes me feel bad to see maybe one of the Lakotas walk down the street, and you can just tell he's trying to put on an act, and he don't really fit in, doesn't really have a cultural background.

## Leading by Example

Having the mentors be sober is really important. They're giving us a gift. They're showing you, here's the good side, and here's the bad side over here, and maybe you're right in the middle, deciding where you want to go. Since they've experienced how it is, they can tell you exactly how it is. And so you really don't need to go and try to find out. I think one of the best ways to prevent drug and alcohol use is having someone who's experienced it tell you, more one-on-one. That stuff you see on TV—like

MTV and stuff—usually ain't going to do a lot. It's got to be right down on you, and the person who's doing it can't be easy on you. They gotta say, "Hey, it's bad for you; what're you doin'?" They gotta be right in your face, letting you know they care about you. 'Cause with this stuff, enough is enough.

When I'm out with my friends, I think about what Sydney and the other mentors have said to me. Like how I don't have to do it. I also think about what could happen if I did do it, and if I don't do it. Then I think about what's happened to people that have done it. I know that if I got into trouble with drugs or alcohol, I would feel comfortable talking to Sydney, 'cause she's so experienced

in it. She knows what's wrong, and how you're feeling, and probably how to get help. She'd be good at that advice. She's kinda here to help me make the right decisions.

## What You Learn in School About American Indians

I don't think we get educated in our culture. It's a white school, I guess you could say. It's run from a white background, and I don't feel they tell the truth about the Indian history, or only partially, maybe. They'll tell you like, hey, the Indian and the whites, they signed

▲ *With Sydney's father, a Lakota spiritual elder (above)*

this treaty and now the Indians are upset. But they don't give you the detail you should have in order to understand it. You know, about how the land is sacred. How the United States didn't honor the treaties; how we were forced to live on reservations. About the boarding schools, and about how we weren't allowed to speak our language or practice our culture. Now they're even making us pay to go onto our own sacred lands.

What they put into the books is one-sided. I think it's wrong that they teach us that way, and I do speak up.

▲ *Protesting a swap of sacred land between the federal government and a development corporation (above)*

I'm outspoken in that way. If I don't think something is right in the book, I'll raise my hand and say it. I think they should have an Indian teach it and maybe rewrite the book and put some insights in it from the other side. It might make people stop and think: Hey, I never knew this; the government did some wrong things here. They shouldn't have done this.

I knew a long time ago from my great-grandmother and my dad about how the government had gone back on their promises. It gets me upset. I think that whoever had the treaties written out and ready to sign, they were not clear; they lied. They didn't do what they said they were going to do. It just makes you angry.

## Spiritual Life and Beliefs

Sometimes I think of my higher power as the first picture of an Indian I ever saw. It was a carving my dad did out of a piece of wood. Maybe that long, about that thick, you know, so that he got a good face in it. Just nice, a perfect-looking face, and it had this big headdress on, and it was an animal—I think it was a buffalo head he was wearing. It was really nice looking, and you could just see the fur. You could feel it. I don't even know if you'd want to name him. It was just this face you could think of, and you could tell it was powerful.

Growing up, though, I was more Christian thinking. I was growing up with the pictures of the white God with the beard and curly blond hair—how you might think he looked, just in terms of how everyone sees him. Then I started to work with Sydney, and we started talking about Wakan Tanka. It's almost a whole other thing. A whole other religion and spirit.

There's more of a feeling for me in the Lakota beliefs. I never really could feel a Christian God; I could more like pray to him, that was it. But over here with the Lakota, here you can feel it. He's here and everywhere. I remember when I was going to do my first sweat, and I was thinking about everything—like the rocks, like if I

▲ *Preparing the stones for the* Inipi *(above)*

was going to mess up. It was my first one, and I was thinking about where and how I was supposed to sit, should I sit by the door or not. If I forget to turn to the right, maybe get confused and turn to the left. The heat was also worrying me. But once you get in there, it's easy. It's just a lot of spiritual feeling, once you're right in there with it all, and everyone else is in there, and you know they're not going to hurt or tease you. Like if you needed to get out or something, they're going to understand. You're not scared to tell 'em.

When I was in there, I was thinking about everybody else. I didn't really think about me or my family as much as I would've liked to. I thought about everyone else's families. Before I went in, they told me to listen to what everyone else has to say while you're in there. Listen to their prayers and their songs. But at the same time, stay in focus with what you're in there for and give thanks and think about your higher power and your Tunkashila. Pray for your grandma and your family.

On the day of my first sweat, I got to meet Sydney's father, and he is a Lakota spiritual elder. He's really wise, and there's really a good feeling to be around him. With everything that he knows, being with him for me was almost like coming in touch with my higher power. On the Lakota side, it's not so much that God is up there looking down at us. God is all around us. And your higher power can also help you stay straight, stay real pure— stay gold, is what I like to say.

## SYDNEY CLAYMORE / mentor, Ateyapi Society

I have an understanding of young people wanting to use drugs or maybe alcohol. Thinking about experimentation is normal. I find the boys are really honest about what they want to do, at least with me anyway. They'll come right out and say, "I'm gonna get drunk this weekend." And I'll say, "Do you really think that's a wise decision?" They'll tell me, "My mom don't care," or, "My folks don't care. So what's it to you?" And I tell them, "I care about you."

If they're having it hard here at school, they'll say, "I'm gonna drop out and be a bum and work at McDonald's." And they'll laugh. I'll again let them know that I care about what they're doing, and that maybe we can do this or that instead to help. Let them know they can do it. I'll encourage them all I can. It takes a lot of effort to be emotionally ready to be able to say, "I'll help you."

▲ *Meeting with Sydney at school (above)*

And that's the same way with drugs and alcohol. Mainly it's just listening. So when they sit there and tell me they drank or they're going to drink, this goes through my mind: Don't shame them, don't point fingers, don't ever say don't. Just really try to understand them and listen.

One of the first things I try to tell these boys is that drugs and alcohol historically aren't part of our culture. We didn't have anything to do with it, a long time ago. It wasn't ours; it isn't ours. So why mess with it? Alcohol was used as a gift or a trading product by the white man. Then it was used to destroy us. Before that, alcohol wasn't an issue. By role-modeling sobriety in the mentor program, hopefully we can show them this, and when they come into our lives and see us working on our recovery, maybe they'll follow along. I tell the boys that I'm sober, that I lead a drug- and alcohol-free life.

Later on they'll question me on how much or if I ever drank. They're very inquisitive. I tell them where I've been. When I do, their jaws drop. It's very important to lead a sober life, because that's what our whole program is based on, role-modeling that sobriety, showing these kids through the mentoring, giving them an education. Whether it's in the form of our recovery, or whether it's education here at school—whatever form it's in—using our Lakota way of life is where the mentoring comes from. They need to see that we are really living what we say, walking the red road. We're being honest with these kids.

Through the mentoring program, the kids will meet someone who's just like them in the sense that we're American Indian, and we're more sensitive to what they might be want-

ing or needing in a specific instance. For example, here at school, the officials have a difficult time seeing where these boys come from. They may not understand the numerous absences or the poor grades, and they might be quick to blame the boy. But all you have to do is go to the home and see why these things happen: There're problems at home. There is drinking, abuse, etc. That child is not thinking about coming to school; he's thinking about what's going on at home.

Then you have a boy who has a problem with someone at the school. He'll say, "I had a problem with so and so, 'cause I'm Indian." They're in this struggle, and when they're faced with conflict, automatically they want to scream racism or prejudice. So I'll ask them, "Well, what does Indian mean to you?" They might say *sweats* and all that stuff, but when it comes right down to it, they have never been Indian; they don't know what it means to be Indian. They might have seen it in a book or a movie. For most of them, that's where they get ideas of what it

is to be Indian. Most, nearly all of them, don't even know one Lakota word. It really saddens me. I want them to find out who they are and to be proud of who they are. Then they can decide for themselves: Was that incident really because of racism, or was it because I was being rude and obnoxious?

To say "I'm American Indian" says a lot. I really need to teach them what being Indian is. It's being a Lakota. It's a way of life, and you do it every day. Prayer, every day—and you are not just praying for yourself, but for the other people: the white man, the black man, the yellow all together, all the colors of the medicine wheel. The first thing I teach them is prayer, because they have no prayer. They might think they do, in a sense, if they make it through the night with all the fighting going on around them at home, or they're praying that their little brothers and sisters will have something to eat. You know that's reality to these kids. So that's their prayer.

I was taught to have prayer a long time ago, and

that's what got me where I'm at. I believe in a higher power, and I had lessons to learn, so that when I was where I am now, I could look and know that this is what I've learned. Even in my darkest hour, I can really rely on my higher power being there. Hopefully when these boys come of age and have their own families, prayer, cere-monies, and spirituality will be a part of their lives. Still going to their jobs or going to school or being part of the mainstream, white society, whatever . . . but keeping our cultural traditions alive. They will still have their heritage intact.

## BRUCE LONGFOX / executive director of Rural America Initiatives

Back in the spring of '92, about fifteen or sixteen Indian men who were into alcohol and drug recovery started to get together. We found we had some common ground. When we sobered up, we all lost our social lives; we lost most of our friends. By trying to be healthy, we became isolated, so we had to try somehow to reach out to a whole different group. We found that we really strongly identified with teens who were having trouble, probably because we have experiences that are real similar to theirs. They feel like they're going through it now for the first time, and we feel like we've been through it too.

As a group, we wanted to give back to the commu-nity. In talking about fatherhood, we came up with a mis-sion: to redefine the role of the American Indian male in today's society. We feel like the role's been lost, continu-ally deteriorating in the time that we've been on the reser-vations. Between the judicial system and the welfare system, we're to the point now where we feel like we've been effectively eliminated from the family. We also feel that the alcohol and drug use compounds all those other problems, so the only rule we came up with is that people have to be pursuing some recovery to join us.

Most of us talk about 12-step programs; others find more traditional methods within our culture, or both. You have to be in recovery. It's real important to verbal-ize that, because it helps with identification. If the boys remember somebody that helped them, at least they'll know that somebody was trying to be sober. If the person is having success now, it's really because they've gone down to their lowest and climbed back up. So the men-tors really understand the process that the kids are just now starting out on.

Redefining the American Indian role is like a circle; it's hard to decide at what one point the circle begins. We see our role as trying to influence the next generation. On the surface, it's a prevention program, but we also see it as instilling identity and self-esteem. If we can accom-plish that, other good things will come along, such as having the kids develop the ability to have relationships.

Right now at home, there's not any relationship they can depend on, so abandonment is a real issue for them. About half of the American Indian families are headed by a single female, and about ninety percent of those are liv-ing in poverty. So most of the kids we're working with come from broken homes. Mom may be working, but she's working at a low-salary job, so the kids experience growing up in what I would say is a dependent system. They know that the rent and the food is basically paid for through Aid to Dependent Children. I don't think they experience what it is to feel achievement. I don't think they experience the process of taking a project from beginning to end. They know how to want, but they don't know how to start the process of saving to get to the goal, of getting the car, or being able to maintain the job.

This is as major a problem as the poverty. It's not only dependence, it's helplessness, too. When you tie that in with alcoholism, you have kids who know what it is to be afraid for people to come home on check day. They know what it is to be codependent, to have their mood be dependent on another person's, whether it is Mom's or Dad's. They check out how Mom or Dad is before they decide how they themselves are.

I think if these kids never learn to trust somebody like the mentors, somebody that's not going to hurt them or abandon them, then they're going to have a real difficult time in any sort of relationship, whether it's with another guy, another woman, a family member, a loved one—any of those relationships. *Intimacy* is the key word, and I think that's what's behind developing a tie and a bond between the mentor and the kids. In order for them to even enjoy life, they have to be able to be intimate with who they're with and with what they are.

I think we have two kinds of shame. We've got cultural shame for being Indian, but we also have individual personal shame for the families of origin, because of the various kinds of abuse that have gone on. I personally think that's why these kids are so angry, so pissed off, and I don't know if they ever come to grips with it. The Red Road people tell us that our complex, whatever that may be, is like an egg. The shell of the egg is anger. The yolk is abandonment, and the center is shame. Part of the process is getting over that center of shame.

I think the biggest thing that we can do to help everybody is to try to define transition curriculum for establishing ceremonies throughout the different stages of childhood and adolescence, making people more conscious of the process. When you go from one level to another, there should be public recognition. There has to be community behind that ceremony. It doesn't do any good to recognize people if the community doesn't have some sort of shared understanding or experience of what that recognition means. Using the *Inipi* ceremonies, singing and dancing, helps to develop identity and also to show that part of maturing. I think you go to the family and start re-creating it in individual families, then eventually it comes back, gaining momentum, and what you're really doing is rebuilding the whole community.

People can help you, but they can't jump you over to the end place. When we work with these kids, we have to remember that we can't fix them, but we can give them tools to cope, and the sacred pipe is the main one, with all the value system that goes around it.

Kiev, Ukraine

# IRINA

18 years old

"When I began my treatment with the psychologists, they helped me remember my childhood, and the majority of my problems originated from there. All the reasons for choice to use the drugs could be called by one name: loneliness. No other reason."

## The Bite of Addiction

When I was fourteen, I started smoking marijuana. There was one man, a friend of mine, he had a lot of marijuana, and it was rather dull for him to smoke alone, so he gave this marijuana to everybody. That's how I started. When I first tried it, I was curious, because I knew a lot of people smoke marijuana and say it is great. Right away I liked the condition of how I felt, so I smoked it regularly for about two years. I was addicted to it right away; a lot of us were.

I was a very sociable person—biggest hooligan in the district [laughing]. I was interested in problems of how to keep my authority high. I needed it badly—the feeling of authority and superiority—because I did not know any other method of self-expression. I was not very skillful in education and was very lazy for studying. But at school or anywhere, nobody could stop me. I did not attend classes for long periods; I dressed the way I wanted, smoked, came without books, left when I wanted. I was sure that I knew everything, that I was one of the cleverest, because I had read all the books for my age and older. Everything I wanted to do, I did. I lived for pleasure.

Things began to involve the police. I started kick-boxing, fighting, and I felt nobody could beat me. I moved to this new school, and at the start, I was very so-

*Standing where she bought and used drugs many times* ▶

ciable. I was on the editorial board of the school newspaper. I had a lot of responsibilities, but after a while I lost interest. I didn't need it. I was the center of attention, and there were a lot of boys around. This was a blind alley for me, because things change in these relationships, which we all go through—I'm no exception. I just didn't understand these relationships anymore. I felt so lonely, and life was very dull, and maybe it was because of that I was smoking marijuana all the time. And the consequence of the smoking was depression.

Mainly it was marijuana that influenced my thoughts that life was not interesting. I was not satisfied or at ease with my old friends, who did not use drugs. They didn't understand me; they had different interests. So I changed my private problems into the problems of getting drugs.

Among my friends, there is a drug-addicted man who was the only one to use liquid drugs like opium. I was interested in that . . . so I used it. I had my first injection when I was sixteen, and it was three months until my next, because I didn't feel the necessity to continue after the first time. I felt so well from the opium that maybe I realized it was bad. I was acquainted with one girl, a hippie painter, who had common interests, so we ran away to St. Petersburg. We spent time with hippies there, smoking marijuana, sight-seeing. After a week, we came back, and when I came back, I didn't live at home anymore; I lived with hippies. I stayed with these friends for a time, and then my sister found me and took me home. My parents were shocked but were so glad that I came back that we talked and they forgave me. They didn't know that I smoked marijuana, and about my life in the streets they knew nothing. This was all during the sum-

mer, so no school at this time. It was such a time when I felt lonely, not at peace with myself, and I could not find my place in this world. So I made my next injection of opium, and I changed my problems again.

I was using injections of opium regularly. I solved the problem of getting the opium by selling it and also marijuana. I would also sometimes get it for free. I would sell personal items, and I was stealing from my sister and parents. My days were like this: From eight, nine o'clock in the morning, I'd get up, wash, dress, make injections, and then go downtown with things to sell. During five or seven hours I stayed downtown, selling whatever and making injections. Then I came back home, make injections, fall asleep, wake up, go out, and come back home at one or two o'clock and fall asleep. That was the regular process.

I was again living at home, and my family knew nothing. My mother explained later that she might have been afraid of drinking, for example, or going out with boys, but never thought of the possibility of drugs. I always wore shirts with long sleeves to cover the needle marks. I would come home late, and my mother would be asleep, so she never saw me sick. My mother knew nothing until I told her myself later.

After a year or year and a half, I tried for the first time to stop making injections, because I felt very sorry for my parents. They suffered because I was constantly running away from home. One time I had been away from the house for three days, and I cut my wrists because I felt so terrible, on the bottom. I was lucky I did not cut very seriously. I came back, and my mother wanted to throw me away from home. I was so worried because she had packed all my things. She said, "Go away," and I had to tell her the truth. I showed her my arms. She was shocked.

I wanted to go away then, but my mother locked the door. Then I explained to her all the symptoms of using drugs. I still used drugs after I told my mother, and sometimes I could conceal it, but now my mother would examine my arms with knowledgeable eyes. I even helped my boyfriend give up opium, but he continued, and I again did opium with him. I could see no other way to live. My mother wanted me to stop, and I explained that it's practically impossible. We quarreled a lot, because she had no idea what drug addiction is. It was something strange for her, some unheard-of topic.

I felt very sorry, because my mother got older. I decided to quit again, and for two months I didn't use any drugs. I used some tranquilizers to help stop the aches of withdrawal. I felt so terrible, emotionally and psychologically, when I stopped. I quit friends who were somehow involved with drugs. I stopped seeing even the boyfriend. It was very hard, but I had no choice.

In time, my friend brought me to this man, always a man [laughing], who had opium and we got together to use opium in great, huge amounts. Pure and sweet. I lost it. I again had same problems with mother and father. I ran away from home again for four months. I lived with new boyfriend and a husband and wife. Very seldom did I go to school, but I did finish, amazingly. We used opium all the time, and then all four of us realized we had to quit opium because we felt so terrible.

After that there was another man who could make amphetamines. The other three had experience of using amphetamines, but I had never. So I started with them, which turned me a little bit crazy. We were all sharing needles, but kept it in the circle of us four—nobody from the outside. Never boiled the needles, only washed from the tap to clean them. There was no sex. No time, no desire. We only made drugs and used drugs. I weighed 106 pounds. It was crazy.

At first my parents tried to find me, but after that they decided to stop. When I came back home, I had not been sleeping for nine days and was in a very bad condition, almost crazy. I said, "Mom, I'm dying." I practically had not eaten food. I looked terrible. I explained to my parents that now I used not opium, but maybe more serious drugs. Mother said, "Stay home and take some rest." I stayed, and I was eating and sleeping for a long time, all the time. My mother was caring for me. I felt better, but I still felt a terrible addiction, so after a week and during the next months, I would leave to make injections, then came back home.

My mother put forward the conditions: Either you'll live at home and don't use drugs, or you'll go away and make injections. I made my choice and decided to use drugs. I felt nothing. I would go along the street and just faint. I was so far away from the community, from the people. I felt as if I were in some glass box that separated me from the surrounding world and those who were looking at me. They saw that everything was wrong with me, but they could not realize what was happening, and because of that they wanted to keep away from me. I understood nothing but getting injections. I did not look like a human being.

One time when I came back home, I asked for help from my mother's friend, a psychiatrist involved in an alcoholic and drug program—how you call those doctors . . . drug counselors. I got a lot of medicine for sleep;

antidepressants, tranquilizers. Also my parents took me to a physician who treated me with hypnosis. Then my mother took me to the Kiev seaside, not far from here, and I ran away from there twice to make injections. I felt so much dependency on the drugs and so uncomfortable with myself.

I came back to Kiev that summer with Father, for some more rest. During this time, I took seventy antidepressant pills, so I would get rid of depression forever [really laughing]. I was put into the special department of hospital for when you are in very bad condition. You know, I took the pills because I was sure I could not live without drugs. I think I was hoping to kill myself.

In the fall, I started working as a waiter in a small Italian restaurant in Kiev. I was seeing my boyfriend again. He sat around with me, saying, "How could you do that? You cannot give up drugs." I had been working two weeks, got money, and bought amphetamines. My mother threw me away from the house because of my adventures. She could not stand to see me dying from drugs. I started buying amphetamines ready-made, so September until January I was using amphetamine and opium without stop. It makes a good balance. Also at this time I was presented with a book about a Czech drug addict, and I read this book and realized that I had to go for treatment. The book has a tragic end because the

man, the hero of the book, became not a human being but like a vegetable. He was twenty-eight. I realized that if I wouldn't stop, I would end up like this.

## The End Begins

I decided to go to a clinic because I felt so helpless and very, very sick. Sometimes I imagined my death. I didn't care very much whether I died or not, but such trifling things like the spots on me, from the needles, stopped me. I had no space for injections left on my body. Of course I knew my life could be better than the way it was. I didn't care, but I felt very sad for my parents. Before going to this clinic, I decided to make several injections, just a farewell. After these injections, I could not get into the clinic because I was bleeding. I changed the appointment and continued to make injections. So appointment comes, and together with a friend I went to the clinic. While waiting for the bus, I fainted, because I was without drugs. I was merely lying on the pavement. A car stopped, my friend worked it out with the driver, and I was taken to the hospital. First they put me in intensive care, and after that I went to the ordinary department. I was there a little over a month.

When I left the hospital, I took the action of contin-

▲ *Buying a loaf of bread (above)*

uing to see and work with the psychologists there. But my condition was not good. So my parents separated me from the surrounding world, didn't call me to the telephone, didn't let me go out, didn't let me walk in the street—all so that I was not to meet the friends. After two months, I was so afraid to go out that I stayed inside. I now feared the people. If I came into the streets, I wanted to escape. Also at this time, I had begun going to 12-step meetings. I heard about these from a friend of my mother's, a physician who had heard about Alcoholics Anonymous (AA) and Narcotics Anonymous (NA) meetings from Americans. She told me she believes there's only one way to get rid of the problem of addiction to drugs and alcohol, and that's by going to these meetings. She told me about a conference, the sixth anniversary of these 12-step meetings in Kiev. I went to this and liked it.

I went to the meetings for one month, about three times a week. Then I started rejecting them, and unfortunately, my old friends began to call me and make offers of drugs. For a while, I could say no. But once I couldn't say no, and I accepted the proposal to do drugs, and that was last drugs I used. I used amphetamines, and there was no satisfaction. I had a bad experience, and I wanted to stop. I knew that I would not move ahead, but just experience the past again, and this does not interest me.

Sometimes my soberness is so unstable that during the day I have to persuade myself that being sober is the right way. I owe myself. I have to do it for myself, for my life, for my health. Then secondly for the family, society, and others. I'm supported by the fact that what I am doing is better than what I was doing. I believe this. I need to remember all these negative experiences I passed

through when I quit drugs. How hard it was for me. How for long periods I was nuts. Once I was coming back home, and I was sitting at the bus stop, and I didn't know what I was doing there, where I was going, what bus I should take—my mind was gone. And when I mention to myself that I might have to pass all this way again, and I would waste all these efforts to stay clean, it stops me from using the drugs.

## Pride and Loss

During the time of using drugs, I was thinking about drugs only. I thought it was very bad, but being a drug addict was my life, and I acted like I wanted it. There were moments that I felt myself the most tough person. I was using drugs, and people are afraid of drug-addicted persons. People would look very suspicious at me; I enjoyed that.

Then came a time when I didn't trust people anymore. Good relationships with my family were broken. I lost almost all my friends, and I lost myself. Society turned back on me. When I was making injections, I never smiled, never laughed. I hated practically everybody. I thought I would live as I want, do everything I want, and I spit on everybody. I lived under constant anger, for everybody, everything, with myself. It was one of the most difficult, black periods of my life, because my life was all lies, hypocrisy, manipulation. I collected all the negative things, and it became my life to be inside all this pain.

There were moments when I thought, I must stop, that I did not want this, but that was only when I was almost dying. I was so sad, but I never thought of quitting. I realized I was dependent, but the drugs were not the

problem. The only problem for me was when I had no drugs. It is very difficult to admit that you have a problem. One of the seven sins is pride, and pride gets in the way. But to admit that you have a problem and need help is the first thing you have to do, and it's one of the greatest things.

In the beginning, I thought that using drugs gave you unlimited creative possibilities. I played guitar, sang songs, recited poems, drawing. I did not understand why you would use drugs if not for some creative activity. But after a while, they took my creativity away. It was an awful period. I found myself incapable, for weeks, of even using a pencil or guitar. This was worse than terrible.

The fear of death became stronger for me, and I realized that it would be a very silly death. In a dream, my mother was drawing a picture of my death, and I am lying dead by a fence. People would come and see me, and then they would look at my passport photo and say, "Quite a different person." I would be buried in some common grave, and worms would be eating me. I would not know what happened with me. Nobody would remember me, because I did not do much. I did not like this end, and I made my choice. I did not really want to die.

## Family

On both sides of my family, there is chronic alcoholism and other problems. The heredity is rather strong. For being sober, there is my sister. She never drinks, smokes, never does any drugs. She is wonderful. In my family, it's a paradox that I had freedom in comparison to my sister. The parents take much care of my older sister, punishing her for bad marks at school. They did not let her go in the street after nine. When it was a New Year's celebra-tion, my mother said to my sister, invite everybody you want, but make this party at home. For me, I went to the New Year's party at a friend's near my home and stayed out for the whole night. My mother said my requirement is every two hours to call home. I was drunk, and friends put me below the window of my parents' apartment, and I was shouting up to Mother that everything is okay. Then friends took me back to the party.

When my mother asked how things were going at school, I always answered, "Everything is okay." And they trusted me. This trust had a negative side, unfortunately. At the same time they did not trust my sister. They thought that she would get into trouble, but she was absolutely normal. They saw that I was more independent, maybe because I could lie. They were not afraid that I would get into danger because of the kick-boxing. Mother said, "I am definitely sure nothing could happen to you." I have thought a lot about this problem. Maybe it would be better to have less freedom, but I only think that now. At that moment, if they had made restrictions, we would have fought. I was very dreadful to the parents.

I cannot ever express how grateful I am for my parents. Father knows I am drug-addicted, and he is very strict, but he helped get me a lot of medical treatment and never reproached me. He was never negative, never saying, "You are drug-addicted, and I spent a lot of money for treatment." No such things. So much support, and I was so lucky not to be alone.

## What Young People in Kiev Need

We grow up in our society living according to this law: If you don't eat somebody, you will be eaten by somebody else. You have to make choice. The majority don't want to be eaten, so it happens they began to eat another person. It's mostly a huge splash of violence. There is indifference from the side of police, from the government, toward trying to change, so things just continue in this way. Of course it gives a lot of young people feelings of hopelessness, if they are in the camp of those who are weak. A major problem is teachers who humiliate children, depending on which layer of society they come from, and on their personal qualities. The teachers act like the weak should die. As you know, there are weak and strong students.

I was in between, skillful but lazy. Those who were below me, who were weaker, maybe physically or mentally, they suffered. I also had something; I was intellectually strong by that time, and I communicated with older students and was in one of the strongest groups in my district. Besides, I could drink, smoke and had a lot of advantages over my classmates. They were just children, and children wilt. So they have nothing to do but drink and do drugs, or they become angry and cruel; there is no other choice. They are just hanging around and using drugs, just to escape. This problem of escape needs to be solved.

Early on for me, I thought anything was possible, but everything changed after I started using drugs. I realized that I had no prospects, no future. No prospect to enter a prestigious high school. My parents are workers, so I could either go to work at the plant or a factory. But I did not want that, and I knew I could do more. But I had no possibility to manifest myself.

One thought comes to my head: that very few young people address psychotherapy. Young people have a lot of problems and don't know what to do about them. It's hard, because very few have thought through how they feel inside. It would be great if in every school there would be a psychologist, or counselor, to whom you could come and share the problems and get help finding your way from this or that situation. I think they have to create some employment centers and some centers for entertainment, especially for young people. There is just not enough of this in our society.

We also need to give as much information as possible about alcoholism and drug addiction. Drugs with young people is a huge problem. The majority of drug-addicted do it just for curiosity and fun, but when they set aside that curiosity, it appears to be too late and they're in trouble. This information should be objective and truthful. Young people should learn the information that alcoholism and drug addiction is a disease, not a sin. Not that the drug-addicted people are not human beings. Not to condemn them; only the drug-addicted or alcoholic can condemn themselves, nobody else.

Young people need to understand that there is a real danger to becoming addicted, and it involves the fact that it is possible for everybody to have this disease. There is no insurance against it. If somebody suffers from this disease, there should be centers where this person could address it and gain professional assistance, qualified assistance. There should be as many rehabilitation centers as possible, and of course it is desirable that they be free, because now it takes money, and people don't have money. If not for my father, I would not have been able to go to hospital those different times.

## Living a "Normal" Life

When I had begun living without drugs, I read an advertisement in the newspaper from a blind woman and called her about cleaning. We agreed on what I should do. I'm trying to begin a normal life. And I sold a drawing to the newspaper. It was very pleasant for me to know that the people like the drawing, but I didn't feel honest. I've done a lot of drawing, and this one is from the past when using drugs. To draw something back then was very difficult, because sometimes I could not take even a pencil in my hand for three months. This drawing is really not professional; now I could do better. I have rather good taste, where there is seldom any in our society. During the period of using drugs, I got much knowledge that could be very useful in normal life, and I want to apply some of these inner qualities, talents, and skills for the benefit of others.

This normal lifestyle seems senseless and dull when using drugs. When you come back into the world, without drugs, the transition period from bad to good takes time. Living with responsibilities, for me, is a problem, because before my only responsibility was getting drugs. Now my struggle is to accept that I have a responsibility. First I tried to say "I don't have any," then after a while I began to think that this thinking is not good. I have to respect the people I live with, whom I make promises to. I cannot do like I did in the past. Once I went to the drugstore for my sister because she asked me to get medicine for her, and I came back a month later with no medicine. Now if parents send me to the shops, I go directly to the shop and buy everything I'm supposed to and come home. I say that these people did a lot for me, and I'm not an animal. If I want to live a normal life, then I

IRINA

do what normal people do. This normal lifestyle should not be analyzed very much, just accepted.

I try to find something pleasant in the occupation, even if I have to clean the bathroom. I try to persuade myself that nobody could clean it as well as me, and that it means somebody needs me. I want to continue these pleasant feelings that somebody cares about me, and that I care about somebody else. I need that. I force myself to do things I don't want to do, and this takes time to become a habit. The hardest one is to really care about myself. It should be natural, but it will take time for me.

In recovery, I started to realize that to live fighting with all the surrounding world is very difficult. No mat-

ter how many drugs you take, it does not help. I also realized nobody cared for me but my family. Even when they saw what was happening with me, they accepted me and helped me. Sometimes the measures they used were very severe, but it helped. When I was discharged from hospital, I had only my family and my friend Viola. I was isolated.

At first, drug-addicted friends called me. I would decline their invitation to meet, and this was a victory for me. It's very difficult when I get telephone calls, and they say, "Help me get drugs." But I found a way for myself—I say to them, "I am too lazy to help you." I tell them that I don't know where to get them, or that I have

to go somewhere, do something. I remind myself I am not using connections anymore, that they can do what they want. After that, it was much easier for me to say no. So, since I've invented that I'm lazy [laughing], I'd better stay home, watch TV, read books, cook, help family. Such a victory—it was celebrated by the family. Once I realized I could stop, that I could make choices, I stopped putting responsibilities on my parents and on the society. It's not their responsibility to keep me away from drugs; it's mine.

I realize that I am sick, and that I'm getting better,

◀ *Handling a phone call from a dealer (at left and above)* ▲

but it still makes me angry. I am feeling myself normal now, but I'm still like a man who was born for the second time and had to pass this way again, and it's very difficult. If children could speak when they were very young, they would say, "This is so difficult, but still we want to speak." That is how I feel. I have the strength to live and be clean, I know I can, but I don't always use my strength. Honestly, I want to be sober. I am willing; I know I can do it. It's not difficult to stop drugs, but staying sober and clean is difficult.

First you remember all the best moments in your life connected with drugs—how good you felt, how funny it was, and how you were so used to living that life. When

111

a drug-addicted person is discharged from the hospital, they come back to the normal world, and they don't know what to do. They're not ready to face the reality, so they go back to drugs, to where they are accustomed. Now when I am thinking about having an injection, I try to think about all the negative things that went on with drugs. I force myself to remember, like when I fainted in the street, when I was not eating, all the deaths around me, and my own slow beginning of death. But this dependent feeling of drugs is sometimes hanging over me for a long time, and sometimes I am in the blind alley, not knowing how to get rid of such despair. Sometimes I am losing sense of what I am doing, and sometimes I think: Is it worth doing this recovery? It's so difficult sometimes that I can't even stand it. I ask myself sometimes: How do people live here in this world without drugs and alcohol? And then I remember all the senselessness of the drug life, and it helps me to restrain. It is very important to remember that you can come back to life, every day, with a chance to live.

## Going to the Odessa Center and 12-Step Meetings

I have to leave Kiev, because it is very dangerous for my soberness, with all of the people hanging around who are actively drug-addicted. I'm crazy about the Odessa drug-addicted that are in 12-step groups, whom I met at the conference. In the Kiev group, the people are not very funny. They are so serious, with sullen faces, and I want to laugh a bit. Odessa groups are kidding, laughing, smiling all the time, and I think that they found a lot of funny things about this disease. It's a very sad illness, but I think maybe they found more fun than sad things. My

mother said there is nothing funny about the problem, but I know if I sit and keep thinking all the time: *I have a disease, and there is a monkey on my back, and how do I live with this problem?* I will go crazy. My decision to go to Odessa is to give myself a chance to stay sober. The center in Odessa is the only center like you have in America—a rehabilitation with the 12-step meetings. So why not go there to get my sobriety started?

Going to the 12-step meetings warms me. At the meetings, there are people who consider me to be worthy of being alive. In our society, there is no respect for and a lot of anger at alcoholics and drug-addicted. My grandfather was a lawyer, and he just expressed his opinions on the problem this way: he said, "Shoot seventy percent of them, and send thirty percent to the special camps." I think this is the opinion of many, many people. Even in the hospital, which is supposed to help the patient, we are not treated like people, but like creatures not even worth existing. It's not looked at as a disease; it is looked at as a sin or moral problem. But at the 12-step meetings, I see I'm human, and the others there are like me; they understand.

Once I was at a concert, and people from AA and NA were there and were so friendly to each other. They name each other brother and sister, and I saw them show a lot of emotions, a lot of joy. I never saw anything like it in the normal world. At the meetings, you can experience these feelings, and a person usually feels not alone, because we share the same problem and solution. At first I thought I would communicate within the family only, and at first it was enough for me. Then when I went to 12-step meetings, I understood there is only one way to go to stay sober, and that is to share your experience with other drug-addicted people. This sharing of experiences at the meeting is so very important because it helps others. Another person could think, "Well, somebody else had such experience, so I would do like this, or I wouldn't do like this." It is important and it works.

Being able to help someone else be sober helps me. It helps because when a person takes care only of himself, it is an act against nature. This care of others is very natural, and if a person who is sick with this disease has no such idea, they would come to it sooner or later, I hope. It's so obvious that if I speak about soberness to somebody else, yet keep making injections and smoking, it would be a lie. I would stop believing in myself, and it would lead to total collapse. So to help somebody, I have to stay sober, and God's thanks, my efforts would be a help to somebody else who would begin recovery from this disease. My dream, not for tomorrow, but for today, is to be sober. Just for today.

**ALEXANDER AKHMEROV, SR., PH.D.** / psychologist in addictive behaviors and director of outpatient programs,
Stupeny Rehabilitation Center

Our rehabilitation center is the only one of its kind in Ukraine, because it's based on the only program that really works—the 12-step program. The first thing we use in the treatment is honesty. We honestly say to our patients that drug and alcohol addiction is a progressive disease of the mind, body, and spirit. When drug and alcohol addicts bring their disease to their doctor, they hope that the physician will help them, and they are mistaken. It doesn't work because the physician's treatment is only for the body, and not for the mind or spirit.

In the past, there were so many bad methods of treatment. Our officials don't see a person in the drug and alcohol addict. So one way of treatment is to isolate them for two years and have them work without salary. They use the labor of these addicts as if they were slaves in a prison. Another method by special doctors is to tell the drug addicts: Please come to us and bring your drug of choice; we will treat you, you will be cured, and you can forget your disease. So the patient does such things, and then they put the patient on a table and make an injection that stops breathing and stops their heart. When the patient is lying on the table, close to dying, the doctors say, "Now I'll make you an injection of your drug; look at this," and they make an injection, and the patient's breathing stops. It's like a clinical death. Then they inject another medicine that wakes up the patient and helps them to live. A drug-addict friend of mine told me he

◄ *Getting ready to listen to Aerosmith with Dr. Alexander Akhmerov*

passed through this process. He said, "I went out from this doctor. I put my hand up, stopped a taxi, and said to the driver: Take me to where I can buy drugs."

It seems to me that to stop using drugs is not so hard. The hardest problem is to stay stopped. Addicts come to our center and say, "With your help, we want to stop." So I say, "You want to stop, or you want to stay sober?" And if they say, "Yeah, I'm ready to stay sober," my next question will be, "Are you ready to change your way of life and your thinking?" If they say "Yes, I don't like to live this way anymore. I want to live sober but I don't know how," I tell them that we can show them how. We have NA and AA fellowship [12-step groups], where people can share with others, showing a new way of life, a sober life.

One man said to me an interesting thing: "I am eight months sober, and I am working very hard. I have money saved, but I have one thought in my mind: For what purpose do I work so hard? I'm sober, so I don't need money, because I'm not using drugs." Maybe an imprint was made in his mind that money is only for drugs—not for clothes, not for food, not for his new child and family. With this thinking and attitude, he needs help to see how he can live sober. That is the work. The first steps of sobriety are a very difficult time period. So we say to them: You must do something every day for your sobriety, one day at a time.

So many are not ready for this. In the mind of the addict is the mistake that they can control their drug use,

115

that they can stop at any moment, if they want. They don't think they need the help of any person. So they say, "I am not asking for help." Some drug and alcohol addicts try to use their own methods to stop and to stay sober. But when all of their methods are not working, which they usually don't, only then do they come to the center and ask for help.

We also treat the family. The state methods of treatment didn't have anything to do with the family, and unfortunately, many have formed in their minds the principle that alcoholism is not a disease, that the drug addict and alcoholic are morally wrong. In our family education programs, a special topic is the influence of the family on sobriety. When you stop the program at the center, your treatment is not ended, only beginning. The problems and difficulties of quitting drugs don't stop; they're right there. As are all problems that you were covering with your drinking or using. So we teach the family how to live with the new man or new woman that comes home sober. They are a new person, so we say to the family, you must change yourself also.

The influence of the family should be positive, but sometimes it is negative because of problems with trust. Imagine the situation, which very often happens, where a young person, newly sober, comes home. Their mother or father says, "Let me look in your eyes. Did you use today or not?" These young people need the trust now. We give them the hope of being sober, and that is how we trust them. I trust that you are trying to stop, that you are trying not to use. We treat them like human beings.

It's very hard to help make changes for young people with this disease, but we must. Every city should have a great number of agencies for psychological help. These centers must have groups of 12-steps for different addictions. The 12-steps could be introduced for an overall way of life, even if you are not an addict or an alcoholic.

I know that our young people and their parents have a lot of problems because we have lost so much of who we were. The ideas of communism are dead. Our children, they studied the religion of communism, and they have three gods: Lenin, Marx, and Engels. It is very hard to give them spirituality, because the great majority of our people are agnostics. So our children look on this life, where the new Russian teenagers are making money, and they think they can be very rich in a short period of time. They don't realize that you still must work hard to get it. I don't think their money is honestly made; it's not my deal, but they are making very fast money. So a lot of our young people think that they don't need to study or to work hard to save.

We have a lot of examples of the other way; you can look at me. I am a Ph.D. in physics and math. I worked all my life, very hard, and now I have two jobs, and my pay is twenty-five dollars a month. So my son, who is twenty years old, says, "I don't need to study. If I study hard, like you, I have nothing. I can buy in Moscow maybe some shoes, boots, or other things, and bring them to Ukraine and sell them and have money this way." It's very easy, and yet it's very hard, and these young people couldn't realize this. The young people are struggling with their parents who worked honestly all their lives and yet have no money; they are poor.

I know that my son must go to dance with his girl-friend, but if he goes to the dances, he must use my monthly salary for only one person. So he couldn't go, and he is saying to me, "Oh, you are bad. Why do you have no money?" Maybe we can help the young person who is not just in drug or alcohol addiction, but who has problems in any case. We must open the helping agencies to the parents, to the children, to the grandparents, because of these serious misunderstandings between old and young. Even in these situations, the principles of 12-steps will be of great help.

Belfast, Northern Ireland

# SHARON

14 years old

# CAROLINE

14 years old

wall" was installed by the British troops to separate the groups.

Peace talks have continued on and off with little success, but during the fall of 1997 and the spring of 1998 a new series of talks that incorporated parties from all sides of the conflict resulted in cease-fires and a new referendum. The possibility for a lasting peace is finally at hand. Back when I was interviewing Sharon and Caroline, however, the future was still dark. I walked and walked in Belfast, understanding less and less. Our talks became my much-needed thread through each day.

Since the late 1960s, violence in Northern Ireland has resulted in more than 3,000 deaths. Labeled the "Troubles," this deeply rooted conflict actually began more than eight hundred years ago, when the British made their first incursions into Ireland. By 1703, ninety-five percent of Irish land was in the hands of Protestant settlers. In 1916, Michael Collins led the Catholic Irish Republicans in a successful uprising that gave the Irish control of twenty-six primarily Catholic counties, now called the Republic of Ireland. The six counties of Northern Ireland, where a Protestant majority lived, remained under the control of the British, and a military presence has been established there since 1972.

Terrorist and paramilitary groups such as the Catholic IRA (Irish Republican Army) and the Protestant UVF (Ulster Volunteer Force) and UFF (Ulster Freedom Fighters) have been fighting for a quarter of a century. According to a 1991 census, more than half of all Belfast residents live in segregated all-Catholic or all-Protestant neighborhoods. A "peace

## Living Day to Day

SHARON: We've known each other all of our lives—fourteen years. We always chum about. It's pretty scary at times, living here in Belfast whenever there would be, like, a series of troubles. When there is a Protestant killed, then you know there's going to be a Catholic killed. 'Cause it's just the way we work—tit for tat. So you're scared, when your father and your uncle and all are going out, in case it be one of them. Anybody's a target. The Protestants could drive up the road and just shoot you for the fact that you're a Catholic, or our ones could drive up the Shankill Road and then shoot them for the fact 'em being a Protestant. It's not right.

Say someone in my family was shot, I wouldn't go or

have someone go and kill a Protestant. I wouldn't try to hurt anybody the way that I've been hurt, because I would know what it feels like. People go through too much pain, and no one else should have to take it on.

CAROLINE: *I'm* not gonna make anybody cry, put it that way. I'm not gonna break anybody's heart— unless we're in a relationship [laughing]. It's really a

retaliation. It's not fair. There's more innocent people being killed over all the troubles than the ones dying in the Irish Republican Army (IRA) or Ulster Defense Association (UDA).

S: And it's them groups that's to blame, because they retaliate all the time, and then they're not getting the harm done to them. It's not their families being destroyed. It's people that's just living a normal life that's being wrecked. It's on the news, and then it's dropped. It's hard, but you have to live with it, constantly knowing about soldiers and all the troubles, people gettin' killed. It's like part of your family. We always lived on Clonnard Street, close to the Falls Road.

When we were younger, whenever there were people stealing the buses and hijacking 'em and burning 'em, we used to think it was brilliant. Like when they hijacked the lemonade van that come around the road. There's a court

at the back of us, and they drove it right up and around and emptied all the lemonade off and set it out for everyone. It wasn't right, because someone else had brought it, see, to sell to other people.

C: [laughing] And then the bread truck—everybody was shoving the bread over their shoulders. Yeah, but it's gettin' worse. That's how it started off. But when you get older, you realize more what's happening around ya, people gettin' hurt for nothing—violence. Life's being taken. Over what? It doesn't make any sense at all. A lot of freedom is taken away from us.

S: A lot of freedom. I mean, this is where we stay. See where we brought you today; we don't even go there. We don't bother. We go about five to ten minutes away.

▲ *After a bombing (above)*

SHARON and CAROLINE

That's the farthest you'll go, where you think you're gonna be safe. There's times you feel very, very trapped. It really agitates you, and you take it out on your parents, and it's nothing to do with them. Your parents try to protect ya. You say, "Mummy can I go?" Your mum will go, "No, it's too far away. There was trouble last night. You can't go, in case something happens." But you go, "Mummy, but Mummy, I'll be all right."

C: But it mightn't be all right. You think you'll be safe, because you're close to your house, but sure, anything could happen. On Sunday, I was going to a wedding party in Ardoyne, and when I let my mum know where I'd be, she said, "Oh, watch it, it's a wee bit risky over there." And then she turned to me and said, "But where isn't?" Like there was a bomb at the corner a while back—just there, not even at the bottom of the street.

S: And my sister came around the corner, and she saw something wasn't right, so she comes around the back into the house, and the bomb went off.

C: Remember our radiator? My sister was on the phone (there's always one of us on the phone), and the radiator comes flying off the mount and hits her.

S: The house was flooded. But you learn to take it. You have to. You're gonna have to live with the soldiers always about. You're in front of them, and you're scared to do and say things. You're brought up not to speak to them, but there'd be an odd time where they'd say to you, "Good morning" and you say, "Good morning" back, because, like, they're being nice to you, so you should be nice to them. But there are some of them you couldn't trust.

C: Like my friend, they used to go down the street to get a smoke, to tell you the truth, and they met a Brit, and he came down to them and offered them a cigarette and all, which I thought was dead weird. Offered them a smoke and stood and talked to them, just normally. He knew where my friend was from, asked: What did he think about the troubles? Had they got any hassle from the rest of the army? Then we'd get other soldiers who if you were walking down the street wearing say a Manchester United [English football team] scarf, they would say to you, "Oh, I'm from such and such," and they would have a conversation with you.

S: But it's scary. I mean, all of a sudden you hear the jeeps pulling up, and the soldiers start running, and you go, "Something's wrong, something's wrong." You automatically go on home and close your door. And you'd tell your mum, and you'd stay in until you hear 'em goin' again.

C: It frightens me; it happens a lot, them coming out of the barracks. They all run. But I do feel sorry for some of them.

S: Some of them, yeah.

C: The thing that made me think was that "Soldier, Soldier" program on the TV. It was about the British army, going to Northern Ireland. It showed you their families, the wives and all, and they were crying. So you say to yourself, they've got families, too, left behind.

S: But that was their decision to be a soldier as well, Caroline.

C: Yeah, I know that's true.

S: They knew what they were gonna have to do.

C: But getting killed too, like when you take it all on to be a soldier.

S: You have to take it all. . . . Sure it's the same, if you're going to be in the IRA or on the Protestant side. You're going to have to take on having to go and kill somebody, and you're gonna have to take on probably getting killed yourself. The way things are now, the Brits stay out of it. They clean up the mess from what the IRA and UDA do to each other, and it's the normal, innocent people who get the problems. The soldiers don't get as much trouble now, but a couple of years back, the Brits and the pellers [police] would get an awful lot of hassle from the IRA. The barracks used to be bombed all the time. It's still pretty regular but—

C: It's usually a petrol bomb now that's thrown. It may seem loud to you, like an actual bomb, a Sentax bomb. But the petrol wouldn't do much damage compared to what was used.

S: You do get a lot of abuse from the soldiers, though. If they want to stop and search you, you can say you're underage. If you're under sixteen, you don't have to be searched. But when you ignore them, you do get a lot of hassle.

C: All the time. Abusive language. It's hard.

S: You'll get called a slut, dickhead; you get called a cunt. When you'd be walking, and there are other people around, and a soldier calling you a cunt or a slut, it really hurts; it makes you feel awful low, embarrassed. You feel that you can't show your face again, because people heard him saying that. You were born right in Belfast, born in Ireland, this is our country. He wasn't even born here, doesn't even know me, and he's a cheek to come over and go "slut."

C: He probably never set eyes on ya before. With all of it, a lot of worrying is involved. A lot.

S: Worrying about something happening to your family or yourself. Gettin' shot. Even to see someone who's been shot or blew up, I mean that's a big fear.

C: You're really scared of what you'll see. It's very bleak, I think. You shouldn't have that many bad memories to put behind ya, . . . and you don't know how far to plan into the future.

S: Personally, I don't look into the future, because of the troubles. The way the killings are going, you don't know, you could be shot. So I don't look in and plan. You don't want to. Most people think, "Ah, I could be dead in the morning." You know what I mean?

C: People say you shouldn't be smoking, but you could be shot anyway. You wouldn't say, "Ten years from now, I hope to be . . ." You don't want to think this way. I don't want to plan something that might never happen.

S: I think we should have the same opportunity as anybody else in any other country. To go on with your life, and know that you'll die yourself in your own way, whenever you're ready to die, but not when somebody's gonna walk out and shoot ya with a gun 'cause you're Catholic.

C: The only thing that should really be stopping you more or less is your health. If you take care of your health, you should have a fit-enough life, but that's not the case. You can have the health, but that won't stop a bullet. You're missing out on a big part of your childhood.

S: You miss a big part of your life, growing up. See for the troubles, you've no time to realize what's happening in your own life. You haven't any idea. There's very little things you can do. Say if you want to go away, you can't go away whenever you feel like it. Time, your childhood, it just goes so quick for ya. What I think is here you grow up too fast, because you have to face the troubles. Say a girl's father's killed. She's gonna have to grow up awful quick to be there for her mother. And you're thinking, "What am I gonna do if anything happens to anyone in my family?" If my father was killed, they took a part of my heart away, my freedom; part of my life's gone now. You don't think about your own life and what's happened in the past for you. It just goes, 'cause you're taking in too much of the troubles. You're so scared that you lose an awful lot, 'cause you've too much else to worry about.

C: As Sharon says, you're too wrapped up on what's happening and what could happen. You're tense, and you're aware, which I feel sometimes is the best way to be, because once something happens to you, you realize, "Oh, can't do this, can't do that." Actually you need to be conscious all along, and not just after something happens.

S: Everyone's aware.

C: Yesterday I had to laugh. My aunt was telling me about my cousin, who's only three. She was with my other wee cousin, and she asked, "Where's your daddy?" and the other girl said, "He doesn't live with me." My aunt said, "He might as well be dead, for she never sees him." And first thing, Dawn turned around and said, "Who shot him?" Normally I wouldn't have thought that much about it. But us talking about it recently made me dead aware, because she's only three. She hasn't started primary or nursery school or anything like that, but yet, she knows.

S: It's like in that book by Anne Frank. I'm always readin' it; it's something I'm addicted to. I really like it. Parts of it are hard to understand, but she lived with the troubles, too. She had an awful sense of fear. They were always waiting for Hitler's people to come kill them. People here are like that, in a way; from one day to the next, you're always waitin' for someone to get killed. But the way she put it in her book, she never let it put her down—the troubles. She had to accept it and just accepted it. She was really—I don't know—she had a lot of courage.

C: Yeah.

S: She waited; she waited until the very end. Till her life got taken off her.

## Going to Holland with the Protestant Youth Group

S: Before we went away on the trip to Holland, we met a few times with the Protestants we would be going with. The first time we met, we went to a community college. There we talked about their way of life, and we told them ours, and they were, like, the same. We had thought, "Oh, they live different from us." But they don't.

C: We met the Protestants, and we just tried to discuss our different opinions, really. Mainly boys started talking about football, which I didn't think was worth it. I think it's more the religions of the teams' backgrounds. In the end, it was all football.

S: You're brought up that way. Protestant, and you like no else but Rangers. Catholic, Celtics. Your daddy taught you to like football he likes, Rangers or Celtics, and you get brought to every match your father's going to.

C: One thing I was shocked at was their football. No, I'm being serious—I support Manchester United, and some of them'ns support them as well. I found that surprising. My favorite football player, right, is a Protestant. And I do get a lot of stick about that, you know, "Oh yeah, you like him, he's a Protestant." The Protestants were saying, "Looks like the Celtics can't even play. They are going to go bankrupt," which they aren't. We got our digs in 'cause we can name more of their players than they can. This was their boys against us wee girls.

It's funny, us young ones being so well educated in the guns and bombs department. I hate to put it like that,

but with the troubles, we are—what would you say?—matured in that way. Then the next thing, we're back to arguing over silly things like football matches. But mainly we just talked about normal stuff, like normal people. On other nights, we were able to talk about pop groups or similar interests. There's not really a big difference between us.

S: I don't understand why we Catholics have to be separated from Protestants with the peace wall when other countries can live with Protestants as their best friends, Protestants sharing houses with them, living next door to them. I don't see why. Every other country has Catholics and Protestants in it; they live together from what I've gathered. There could be one Catholic standing on the corner with Protestant wee girls, and no one would be able to pick her out.

C: But yet, as we said, when you're gonna meet Protestants, you'd be very, very nervous. You'd say to yourself, "I'll be one Catholic," you know what I mean. But meeting with the Protestants is helpful; it lets you have a clear picture of them and their lifestyle and things like that.

▲ *The Catholic and Protestant youth groups meet (above).*

S: The Catholics, the ones who went on the trip were saying, "Protestants, right, we'll get them; we'll give 'em a beating." That sort of attitude. You know we were like "They're not us, they're different from us." And then we went, we meet them. The first time we met them we—

C: —were able to talk, on the trip, about, like, the way they celebrate their twelfth of July holiday. **[The anniversary of the Battle of the Boyne in 1690 is celebrated by Protestant marches through Catholic neighborhoods every year on July 12. In that battle, the Protestant William of Orange defeated the Catholic James II's attempt to regain the British throne.]** We find out what they do for it, and tell them what we think. We don't like the way they do it, because they're allowed to march through Catholic areas on the twelfth of July, and we're not even allowed to march. We remain in our areas, but they're allowed to march through ours.

S: They told us they don't have to go to chapel, they could go if they want, and other things about the religion that I didn't know anything about. Like communion, or being baptized, or what prayers they know. But really, it's their life, same as us. It's just the same.

C: It all changed on the trip. . . . Sharon fell in love. She went out with him for three weeks.

S: A Protestant boy, yeah. Used to get a lot of stick because of it, like, "You're a pretty bad Catholic, and you're going out with a Protestant; ah, come on, you'll do better than that" and all. My boyfriend knows, told him the day

I came back. If we were turning back time, I would do it again. Meeting them, it all really changed. The first time we met, our opinions just changed, and we realized then that they were the same people as we are. We don't understand each other's point of view, 'cause we never really had the chance to talk. We were amazed when we came back from the trip. The first thing we see was, we see the British soldiers. We got off the plane, and got on the bus, and drove out just a little bit, and there was a checkpoint and we couldn't get over it. We hadn't had that, and then all of a sudden it's back again—the place, the soldiers always being around you. The tension comes right back.

C: What I would love to know is, are the soldiers all Protestant? I always thought that they were, and I thought they were over here to keep control of the Catholics, and that there was no soldiers on the Protestant side. That's the way I always thought.

S: But when we went away with the Protestants, we found out they have soldiers on their side, and they hate the soldiers as much as we do.

C: Which I never—

S: And we were really shocked. When we met the Protestants, we really get on with them dead well. Like when we got back from the trip, we went ice skating. It was mostly Protestants that were there at the place, and they wanted to fight with us. The young Protestants that were with us said, "We'll back youse up." So they were taking our part against their own people, and that felt good for us, 'cause we thought, "The Protestant people are on our

side as well." They do care about us, in some ways. They're not all bitter, and I don't think all Catholics are bitter, either.

## Shankill Road Bombing

**In 1993, an IRA bomber died in a premature explosion that claimed several innocent Protestant lives in a fish shop on the Shankill Road.**

S: When it happened, I was just shocked and saying to myself, "It's not right," and what with us being away and meeting with the Protestants, we thought, "How're we gonna face them again?" For them knowing that our ones went and bombed them, whether there'd be children there or not. They're killing innocent children, . . . and what if it was the ones we went away with? What are we gonna do if we know them? See, if it would've been the ones we went away with, we couldn't have went to the funeral even. You couldn't have marched on the Shankill Road in the funeral, because people would have bothered you straight away for being Catholic.

C: And then on the news, we saw one of the girls we went with on the trip to Holland. It was her friend who was killed, and she was at the funeral, and she was laying flowers. It was terrible, and it was so hard to take in.

we can be, like it was nothing.

C: And the IRA man ended up killing himself. It's a waste of lives. Sometimes with this, you have to watch what company you're in to say things. You can't like, start in anywhere and say, "Oh, I think that bomb was terrible and all," because there'll be people around ya who disagree with you, and whose parents are closely connected with it all.

S: 'Cause you knew that they knew the young girl that was killed, and she was about thirteen or so. There you go, she didn't even get as much of a life as we get, but for dying so young. I say, we were all in a crowd one night, just after the Shankill bomb, and I said, "Wasn't it terrible?" And they were just, "There's another couple of Protestants gone; there's a few less you have to worry about." But I said, "You don't look at it that way, because what would you do if it was your younger brother or sister that was killed? Your mum or dad?" Nobody could look at it, "Gee, sure, they're only Protestant; sure, what's the difference?" 'Cause it's not that way.

They were Protestants; we never knew them, but it still means something—there's another life gone. Children and all were killed in that bomb, for the sake of them being Protestants, and what's the sense in that? They're not getting another life. Then to see a mother on TV and all, her family in an awful, awful state, just for the fact that the IRA needs to walk up on the Shankill Road and bomb it, and going to see how big

S: See, when the Shankill bomb went off, they says it was going to be an awful lot of retaliation by Protestants. So me and my boyfriend never went out then. We used to sit in all the time, and when he went home, he used to phone me so I would know he was okay.

C: And then all the Catholic bars got mass cards with death threats. I thought that was terrible. At night you were scared to go out; everybody was. They said on the news that after 6:00 P.M., there's gonna be war. So everybody was in their house. You'd run to the shop and run home again. Be back in two minutes. A cat run out in front of me, a simple cat, and frightened the life out of me.

S: 'Cause you know there's always someone out there that's looking for a target. After the Shankill bomb, they says anybody walking on the Falls Road is going to get shot. So what it's all going to be is that they will get one of ours, and then we'll kill two more of theirs. None will let go. At the time of the bombing, when everyone was screamin' and all, the Protestants on the TV were saying they're coming over here to shoot us. So I says I thought we should have someone from the Catholic side give our point of view, because so many of us were really like, "It shouldn't have been done, people dying for nothing."

I says to my mum, "I'm going to the TV people and bring them over here and let them hear about what we think of the Shankill bombing." Tell them that it affects us and hurts us as well. I didn't understand why they just wanted to put the burden onto us, 'cause we couldn't take it as well, their people being killed. But they wanted to pass the burden, and I don't see why. We have lost an awful lot of our people as well; it's not just the Protestants gettin' killed, it's us as well. All of us end up suffering. When a Protestant gets killed, it's not like you don't feel for him, even though he's not part of our religion. We feel for them as well, but I don't think they realize what or how we feel.

C: It's only a religion that's the difference; they're still people, so they have feelings. And, like, a lot of us have Protestant and Catholic relations. Both sides are saying, God, religion, but they're fighting over it, which I think is strange. You're supposed to have that gift and all, from God, and yet you're actually killing people over it.

## Solutions: "We've Never Been Asked"

C: I think that there's more people who want peace and who want to get together than all the members of the UDA, IRA, and all the rest of groups. We are the majority.

S: Why should they be stopping us?

C: There's nothing to put faith in right now.

S: It's gone on so long, and too many people have been killed, so they're hardly gonna just say, "Let bygones be bygones."

C: Like, say if the IRA called a cease-fire and sat at the table—that would be a start. But there's no start right now.

S: If, say, the IRA wanted to call a cease-fire, they would've done that long ago. But I don't think any of them want it. So you stay frightened, and it makes you think that you want to move when you grow up. There comes a time when you can't take it anymore, and you explode. There should be an organization—I'm not just saying for young people, I mean for old people too, for everybody—because the troubles are such a big part of people's lives. It's very important that people should have someone to talk to about it.

Nobody makes an effort to try to explain the troubles. Honestly, I think it should be taught in school. Say a close relation of yours is killed, and you're just told that it's because he's a Catholic. But you've no understanding why. We don't know why the troubles started; I haven't got a clue. You pick up bits and pieces. To start it off right, it should be through school, and the school should let us join with another Protestant school and talk about it, discuss the troubles. And then, say, write out what we think, and the way we feel, and send these words away to the government, get it to TV news or something like that, so people will say, "Children are doing that, because

they're sick of the troubles. They want people to know how they feel, 'cause they don't want it happening."

C: I think a lot of people in school would give it a try, and fair enough, everybody'll not make it every week, or stick at it for the whole time, but at least they'd be told more about it all. I just think we should know more background on, let's say, their religion, 'cause that's what we would argue and discuss with the Protestants. If you're going to argue with somebody, you should know what you're arguing about. 'Cause you get to speak out, and say what you want, and let other people know how you feel. I'm sure you'd find other people feel the same as

you. When you bottle everything up inside—

S: Like with the Shankill bomb, it wasn't mentioned in school.

C: Maybe it was at assembly. "I'm gonna pray for the people who were killed."

S: But the teacher doesn't go, "What do you think of what happened?" Or, "Did you know anybody?"

C: Nothing like that. And then you feel you're not important. That you're not a big part, and what you say

SHARON and CAROLINE

doesn't matter. But what you have to say *is* important.

S: I think we need someone to trust. If something goes wrong, they'll be there for ya, and they're gonna listen to ya all the time. I think we'll need that, and we'll need a big miracle. In a way, people would say the day Jesus worked miracles when he was young: Why can't God work miracles to stop the troubles now? You will hear people saying that, blaming it on God.

C: To get good things, you have to try. You know things don't come true without that.

S: You can't click your fingers and it's gonna happen. Everyone has to pull in together, work together. But we young ones don't get a say. No one really does, except for the head IRA man, the UDA man, the government, you know, the parties. They get the biggest say.

C: We feel as if, now we're talking, people will read it and understand our point of view. Normally we don't get asked our point of view, because we haven't got the power.

S: We're too young, and they're not going to listen to us 'cause we're children. "You don't know what you're talking about; we're older, we've lived with it more than you two have, we've seen more things than you. You just sit there and keep quiet. You're only a child." And I don't believe that. I think we should have a say.

C: It makes you very angry not to have a say.

S: Well, they should understand more what children feel like.

C: You have to know you're talking to someone in confidence. I hardly think they would take us seriously.

S: So you wouldn't have the nerve to go and ask for things, 'cause you think, "Oh no, it's too much; I can't ask for that. I'm embarrassed, what am I gonna do? They're not even listening." But you should have a right to ask.

C: The young people could say, "I'm not joining the IRA," or if you're Protestant, the UDA. Just stay clear. Some of the younger boys, especially, want to be with these groups for control and power.

S: I know, they think it's, like, hard, and people gonna pay heed to them, be scared of them. But what needs to be done is that the head of the organizations, whoever they are, should go and tell the police to make a secure area, and these head men should be able to sit in the same room and discuss it right.

C: If they've so much power to kill people, have they not got enough power and control to talk? It must be proved first that they can be men without having to bring weapons in.

S: They're brave enough to kill innocent people—you know, go up on the Shankill Road and kill somebody—they should be brave enough to sit with each other and talk. They need all weapons confiscated—guns put down. If it's gonna be done right, I think the British soldiers should have theirs took off them as well. If there's not a gun in it, then I think they'll be some trust, 'cause once someone has a gun and shoots it, trust is over.

SHARON and CAROLINE

C: What I don't understand is how anybody could live with themselves after shooting somebody, then go home to your wife and children and eat with them and watch it on the news.

S: People who are in the IRA are saying they are fighting for a United Ireland, so first we find out who the people are that want it from both Protestant and Catholic sides, and if that's what they want, then we would call a cease-fire and try to have all the weapons removed. Then we would try, in say a year or two, mixed schools—Catholic and Protestant students together. In the meantime, we'd have the parents, the older ones, at meetings and discussing things. But I think they should go for peace first, because I think the government is trying to work it too fast. They want it to be like a United Ireland and then the troubles will be over. Right? You say the word, and that's it. But you can't have it like that. If it's gonna be a United Ireland, we might as well have it right and let Protestant and Catholic be neighbors, if they want. And then we'll have to have a group where people could go and be asked questions—"Well, what do you feel like with a Protestant living next door to you?" They can't just have Protestants move into Catholic area, and Catholics move into Protestant area. There's gonna have to be a lot work before this.

C: But if you say now, I wouldn't want to go to school with Protestants in this present situation.

S: Right, 'cause I think it should be took step by step. I don't think integrated schools should be, like, now—no. I wouldn't go to an integrated school. Only if there was peace, and then I would let it run for a year or two to see what way it works.

C: Well, I would go, but not for a while anyway. I don't know, maybe. But I think everybody should have a choice. Instead of just going to Catholic or just going to Protestant school, you could choose what you wanted. There are some integrated schools. . . .

S: Yeah, but they're more for people out in the country, and places where they have money. Not right in Belfast.

C: They're not on the Falls Road.

S: I don't think an awful lot of people's mothers would let them go, for a while anyway. Because the parents would have to meet first, and the parents would have to do something together as well. The way we were brought up, going to school with Protestants is like, out of the question. I wouldn't go to school with a Protestant. I mean, I don't know. I went away with them, and that's one thing. But say we have a United Ireland. Would our peace wall come down? You know we'd still be here in the Catholic area, and they'll be in their area, and then we'll go to school together, and then they're gonna go back and we're gonna come back here. What's the use? I don't think that wall there will ever come down.

C: But I think if you can go to school together, you can live together. Whenever, say, there's peace for a while, and then the next thing there's bombs and people gettin' shot, you feel hopeless. What's the point of it, anymore? You do get angry. I think we need more of the cross-community work. I know it helps us. Why could it not help other people? I think the Clonard Youth Club is do- ing all they can. I believe that, 'cause they're bringing the two groups together.

What we need is something to look forward to, 'cause I think if you're given something, and there's some- one there, able to tell ya, "If the Catholics and Protes- tants get together, we will be able to do this." Say even something stupid like being at a disco in the middle, be- tween the Shankill and the Falls. Somewhere in a neutral area. It'll be really, really good if you did have a friend who was Protestant that you could get in contact with. 'Cause say if somebody close to you was killed, that you'd be able to go and talk to that person, and they'd be able to tell ya how they'd feel about, say, their Protestants doing that on ya. Don't you think that'd be good? You'd see two sides of the story.

S: The ones we went away with, we very rarely get to see outside of the youth groups. We met them in the town a few times, 'cause all of a sudden we just seen them and talk to them for a while. But you're even scared when you're in the town, in case somebody recognizes ya, 'cause you're not meant to be talking. Like when we come back from Holland, we met the Protestant girls an awful lot, and then they told us they were warned to stay away from us, that they couldn't meet us unless it's with the youth groups and the leaders.

So I think we would have to have groups for the younger and the older ones, like the parents, for them'ns to go and have people to talk to. Otherwise us young ones will be all good and ready for everything to work well for Ireland, and then we'll go home and not get the

support. But I don't know if we'll ever live together.

When my mum was a child, she used to go to her granmee's house, and she played with two Protestant girls. One day she was playing with one of the girls, and their dog and the wee girl come up and says, "No, I'm not playing with her—she likes the Pope; we don't even like the Pope. She's one of them people goes to mass and all." My mum says, "To this day, I can't get over her saying that to me; that'll always stick in my mind." The wee girl, you know, must have heard it in the house. It was what she was brought up around.

C: It would be very interesting if we got the chance to talk with Protestants about how we feel, how to make changes—to see their point of view. 'Cause you'd never talked to them like that before. You get uncomfortable just bringing it up, where if there was something set up to help us, especially for that, it would be good.

S: Like on the trip, there was times when you were sittin' and there was nothin' to talk about, but you would love the chance to be able to say, "What do you think of the troubles? Hard for me to live with it. Do you think you can cope with it?" I don't think anyone would be brave enough to bring it up. The youth-group leaders didn't bring it up, either. I think it could've been brought up by a leader, 'cause leaders are there for guiding, but the Protestant leader was gettin' his digs in about Catholics all the time. So you were scared, bringing it up. I didn't want to put myself there. That's why I didn't mention it.

C: I think that if you do have these discussions in the cross-community work, both sides should be told that this would be discussed. Because if a Protestant's sittin' here, and the next thing that comes up is religion or the troubles, he'd be very shocked. If anyone was to come up and ask me what religion I was, I would panic; I really would. And you would look for clues on them, like if they're wearing a Celtic scarf, then you'd say "Catholic." You'd feel okay about saying it.

S: The only thing you need is communication. You wouldn't be able to do it on your own—just walk over to the Shankill Road, straight in, and rap someone's door and say to them, "I'm a Catholic, and I'm just asking, what do you think of the troubles, do you mind?" You would literally get kicked out of the Shankill. So together we would need a group that could try to come to a conclusion about trying to stop the troubles.

C: You know this is the first time we've really talked about this.

S—C: Talked about solutions, yeah.

S: The youth club is getting done up. There's no upstairs in it now, but it's been extended off as well, and there will be all these new rooms in it. There's going to be a conference room. So in that room could be a discussion, one night a week, to try to talk about solutions. I think an awful lot of people would come. We could put that to Crawford, to ask if we could have that room.

C: You gonna need somebody to be there to talk, to give us a push for our confidence.

S: You could even put up a poster, like, to get names, and then see how many people would be interested.

C: It would be interesting. People would be coming out and talking about it, and then other people saying, "Okay, I might go." You know, things like that. 'Cause I think it's a topic that there's no definite answer to, really. I don't think there's anybody in the power at the minute. There are no leaders.

S: That's right. Better to have us, for the young ones' point of view. Say you maybe get five people to come to the group. And then you—

C: Bring them off the streets: "Come on, you have to listen to this." [laughing]

S: It would be doing something. Thinking about it, that's why I would hate to leave Belfast and live somewhere else. You want to stay here, but there is no opportunities. But I'll stay for it, because the younger ones is gonna grow up, and then they're gonna have to take the burden on themselves, and I don't think it's right that they should have to take that burden of all the troubles. You have to start something that helps solve the problem.

C: It mightn't do anything major, but it's a start and you have to start somewhere. That's the way I look at it.

## CRAWFORD FITZSIMMONS / director, Clonard Youth Group, Clonard Monastery

I live in an outside area where there is very little hassle. No barrier of security groups, for example. You see young people there who can cope with adults and cope with schoolwork and things like that. Here in Belfast, it's a totally different setup. Now I can't prove that it's because of the troubles, but that's the only thing different between here and where I live. Growing up in the troubles has made these young people more animal-like. I hate to use the word, but I've used it before, and it's the only way I can think of it. They live on their nerves, on their basic instincts. They live day to day in sort of a protective mode. Anything threatening or unknown frightens them, or anything new. Without thinking, they dive and protect. Life becomes the challenge of living within the confines of your area only. I find that impinges an awful lot on the work that we do here. We're constantly motivating them to come out of that mood.

The youth club is basically recreational, for a start. We try to work with the schools, and if the schools are doing something, we don't do the same thing. We complement it. We also work with employing agencies and ask them to help. We go and say to them, "Help them a bit, give them a break; you won't be disappointed." Sometimes our young ones get stereotyped as coming from the Falls Road. But some of the employers did take a chance, and it's worked out.

And then it's talking to the kids at the club, and letting them know that they have skills and talent. Helping them to understand their mentality, ·that they can't survive all their lives in that one area. They have to work, they have to get a job, they have to go to the doctor's, which

is all outside the area. It's getting them to appreciate that and to move 'em forward from that. I'd argue their world's been too sheltered, and they need to be challenged, because if they're not aware of their fears, they're gonna walk into trouble. The important thing is getting them to realize that they have the skills to cope.

Cross-community becomes a part of it, but it's still only a small part. We would love to have more regular contact with Protestants, but we don't have the opportunity. We can't walk down the road and cross the Peace Line and into the Shankill Youth Club. If we were able to do that, we'd have regular contact every night of the week. But that's not a possibility. First of all, we wouldn't get permission from the parents of our own members to go. There are many, many factors that would try to prevent the young ones from meeting. But we have begun.

How that came about was during the summer. There's the Peace Line, behind the club, and our members were leaving here at eight o'clock, and we weren't seeing them again that night. We wondered, you know, what's going on? We took a look around, and we saw them throwing stones and such over the Peace Line at each other. The youth leaders from the other side of the wall were saying, "They're throwing stones at each other, and they're so close. Why can't we build a program that is a bit more constructive than just throwing stones?"

Now it took us about two years to start and build that program, because I was basically afraid. I didn't want to be the first person in the area that says, "Come on, let's work with young people from the Shankill." And the

leaders at the Shankill Youth Club had the same problem. We got help to negotiate a safe passage with some of the leaders, and it started. Within a year, we realized what we were doing, and we saw that we were playing it safe. The young ones, nine or ten, had very little hassle, and they were basically happy enough to play football and everything like that, but we weren't addressing the issues. And we said, "Let's go attack, like head-on, and get the older ones." What we saw was that they needed something in common.

They are quite prepared to sit here among themselves, in the youth club, and talk about the problems

▲ *Sharon at her job (above)*

they have with ones on the Shankill and vice versa. But it's actually getting 'em together to talk that's the problem. And that's when we decided on going to Holland. In three weeks of concentrated work in Holland, were they to fight and argue with each other, they would still have to smell each other. The young people were able to cope with each other in Holland without the pressures of their own communities. When they come back to Northern Ireland, you know, it was very difficult for them, and given that the Shankill bomb happened shortly after they came back, that only exacerbated the problem.

I would've liked at that stage to have gone to the Shankill Road and be with them, the Protestants. But I didn't. And I feel a tremendous letdown personally that I wasn't able to cope with that myself at the time. I tried to argue with myself that if I had gone, some people from the Clonard area might have heard that I had been there, and they would've been saying negative things about it. But that's only a cop-out, you know. Basically I haven't got the ability to go there. I couldn't go as a youth worker and be seen there. At that particular time, I'm sure Sharon and Caroline told you, there was an awful lot of hostility. The things you heard on TV and radio, you know, "If I had a gun, I'd go to Falls and shoot the Catholic people."

But two months on, when the Clonard and Shankill groups were beginning to re-form, the young people of the Shankill surprised me by saying, "We want to meet the Clonard ones again. We want to continue that contact." Not all of them, but seventy percent saying, we want to meet. So I felt a terrible heel. Here was me withdrawing because of the fears, although they were legitimate fears. Again that fear is preventing us. I mean, I knew I should've been there. It bugs me to this day that I didn't go, because I know now that we would've been in a better position working with the Shankill group and with the knowledge that we had gone and sympathized with them personally.

But the way the bombing was portrayed by the media wasn't really the truth. What I am told now is that the individuals that said those things at that particular time had to be sought out. The people the newspeople were meeting on the Shankill first were saying, "It's a tremendous tragedy. We regret it; we don't blame the Catholics," you know. And that's not what the media set out to look for. So they had to keep going, on and on down the road, until they found someone prepared to say, "I want to go to the Falls Road and shoot a

Catholic." That was the broadcast. I would consider myself open-minded, but yet I was fooled by that, and it affected how I reacted. But now, having talked to the people of the Shankill, I very much regret not going over there. So if I have those problems coping, it's even more difficult for young people. I'd love to go back to those days with this knowledge and be able to cope with that fear.

Now on a grand scale, we might have little to show for our cross-community work, if we're being honest. But from my point of view, this is not negative, because what we have done is shown that young people, from Catholic and Protestant areas of Belfast, taken out of these contexts, can live and work together just like ordinary people. For our own setup, it meant that from now on we'll be looking for more regular contact at neutral sights here in Belfast. We are adamant that the more contact they have, the better they are for it. That's the only way. And I would argue, because of this, for the integrated education system in Northern Ireland, because I believe that the only thing preventing these young people from working together is the fact that they do not meet.

When they did meet, they were able to cope with a lot of problems, which were big problems for adults but for them weren't very big. I don't think a lot of adults can come out of this way of thinking, where if they're Catholics, they're true-blue Catholics. If they're Protestants, they're sure to be true-blue Protestants. The basic fear of each other is ingrained in them so much, they can't cope. The hard-line denominational beliefs have at times a very negative effect.

What we're saying is, "Let's look at it from a Christian perspective." If we can sort of take out all the harshness that exists in being a Catholic or in being a

Protestant, you find a solution whereby you become a Christian.

I can't say in four or five years' time, when these young people become adults, that they're gonna start saying, "Cross-community is the future." What we're trying to do is create a future for them to live in peace and to understand what it is to live in peace. I still wonder whether some of them will be able to cope with peacetime. There is an optimism among the older young person not to tolerate the troubles forever. I think it's at the stage where some of them have gotten together, and they are saying "We must have a future for our children. We're not going to allow this to go on, and we're going to work hard, so they don't have to live the way I lived." Now, we're talking about only thirty or so young people that we are working with so far, and there're hundreds of young people out there on both sides. It's a drop in the ocean, but there is value in a small group. We planted a seed. So we did that this year and let that group go, and next year we'll take a different group. Year after year, it must have an impact.

**PAUL SWEENEY** / director of Northern Ireland Involuntary Trust

I don't think in Ireland young people are all that liked, which is a very, very general, sweeping statement. If you looked at young people as being the lifeblood of any community, the ability of any community to replicate itself, to build a future, then a society coming up through that ethos would have a very dynamic approach to young people. But the reality historically is that Ireland exported its young people. The economy, for whatever reason, was never dynamic enough to sustain the level of the population of young people. So what happened is that young people have emigrated from Ireland, primarily to America, where they made a significant contribution. That was a safety valve, and a way in which society was able to flush out its system. Generations of young people which if they'd stayed in Ireland, perhaps could've gone in a number of directions.

Now the safety valve of emigration is no longer a serious option. The people who went over to America years ago were invariably from, if I can use this term, a peasant background. For the most part, that has changed quite a bit. Now you have from Ireland the economically mobile, the highly educated, the well-trained, who have looked not only to America and Canada, but Europe and other parts of the world. And certainly the Irish educational system for the economically mobile is wonderful. But left behind increasingly is this disaffected, unskilled, poorly educated sixty percent of the young population, both north and south, for whom emigration is not an option.

Complementary to that is the fact that Ireland, north and south, is a very deeply Christian society, and a very traditional society as well. It's always been resistant to young people, who have been perceived, generation after generation, as being a threat to the moral makeup of the

pounds a day to run the security forces in Northern Ireland, but if peace broke out today, sadly that money would not overnight be diverted toward social programs. The state will meet, whatever it costs, what the IRA throws at them, but the state will not think about putting the same money into programs that would help the area grow.

nation. So what frustrates me most then, about Ireland, is that I don't think we like our young people. And a frightening way of looking at the consequences of this lack of response is that you end up with a very apathetic society. And the moment the society becomes apathetic, the more that the animated few, particularly the zealots, call the shots.

But we must never give up hope. That is really important. I think that history has dealt our young people a bad hand, and I think that they are innately a very talented, colorful people with enormous potential. In a different society, they'd be winners; they'd be champions. I'm calling for a new deal so that they are guaranteed some meaningful stake in society. By age twenty-five, each person would have a foot on some ladder that's giving some kind of meaning to their life.

The scale of this place is such that you can actually do something meaningful; you can actually target resources with precision. It costs hundreds of thousands of

But the greatest threat to democracy is indifference and apathy. It's not necessarily the IRA, soldiers, UDA. These groups only become a symptom of a society that's indifferent. The sad thing is that not enough people are dying, right? It doesn't impact acutely enough on everybody's lives. There's a tremendous comfort factor, even though the violence and deaths have been of a particularly pernicious and brutal nature. The violence is focused in certain communities, but that enables a major amount of people to be disengaged.

So you have this pathetic kind of time-warped war going on that's containable, frustrating, convenient, and exhausting. For some, it's more preferable to let it drag on rather than to challenge and get a new way forward. And the very people that could do something about that are the young people, the future generations, and they are not always inclined, because they are not empowered to bring about that change. They are being robbed of that chance.

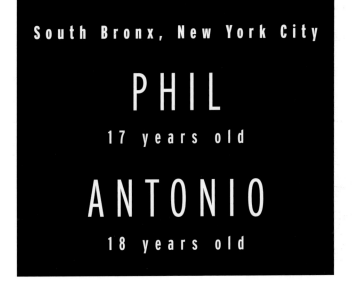

# PHIL

I was goin' to Morris High School in the Bronx. I had a lotta problems, fights almos' every day. And just, I got tired of it, and my moms got tired of it. I was like, "Look, I need a change; this environment is not doin' nothin' fuh me." Those classes was wild, 'cause people throwin' shit, spittin', taggin' up on the walls, talkin', screamin', and people was doin' that he-say/she-say stuff. I was havin' mad problems, yo. I was confused, worried and shit, because I was failin' my classes. When I was in junior high school and elementary, I always did well—not real well, like a nerd or somethin'. But I'd do my thing, 'n' get outta the class, and pass. Now I was, "Damn, if I don't get these credits, I ain't gonna get outta the ninth grade." I wasn't the type that wanted to get left back. You know what I mean?

I was sayin', I only got four mo' years to go, so I'm tryin' to bust this out. But these teachers, givin' all this work, not explainin' shit to us, an' expect us to do it. I could see if they explained it, "Look, this is how you do dis . . ." But I don't know how to do it; I don't even know where to start. The teachers never disrespected me, but they didn't respect me. I brought it to one teacher's atten-tion, and then my pops came in, and it was a big shit. After that, the teacher paid more attention to me than anybody else in the class, and I felt that wasn't right either.

## I'm Outta Here

All the distractions got me into fights. I was the type that never backed down. I would just be like, "Whassup, let's do this!" Growing up with my father—my pops was in the army, Vietnam—he never communicated wit' nobody, 'cause everybody in the war was out to get him. He taught us, 'cause we livin' in the same process: "Yo. Don't even talk to that person. If he tries t' disrespec' you, just hit him." But that's how my pops grew up. Even though now he's calm, he chills and tells us to chill; when he was younger, he didn't care. Just like, when we was young, we didn't care.

I don't walk in the middle of the hallways in that school, because you cou' always get caught up in the mix. Everything happen in the middle. So I was just walkin' one time by the wall, and this guy is leanin' up against the wall, so I move out a little bit 'n' pass him, and he goes "Yo, money, why you walkin' so close to me?" I turnt around. I was like, "You talkin' to me?" and he was like, "Yeah, I'm talkin' to you." You know, tryin' to be smart. I was like, "Yeah, I'm talkin' to you! Yo, first of all you shouldn't even be raisin' your voice at me, 'cause I'm a bus' somebody in the ass." That's 'cause I was stupid; I was young then. We was ready to fight, but they stopped it. Later he was outside waitin' fuh me, and I was like, "Let's go." That's how I used to think, but now I'll try to avoid alla that.

*Phil with his father* ▶

One time, I was sittin' in my class, and everybody just ran out the room 'cause there was a fight on the second floor. Insteada runnin' away from the fight, people was runnin' to it, and some kid got stabbed in his head. He was bleedin' all over the floor. I was like, "I gotta get outta this school, man, 'cause if I get killed in this school, somebody's gonna try to get revenge, you know, family-wise."

So I left Morris. Basically I just stopped goin'. I wasn't gonna be goin' to a school that is distracting me totally and takin' my mind off the goals I'm tryin' to achieve. Since I was young, I always wanted to be an architect. I draw every day, draw anything. I love it. It plays an eighty-percent role in my hundred-percent life. So I realized I needed to make a change. And, in a way, I realized I was part of the problem, 'cause I was like "Damn, man, if I just mind my own business and do what I gotta do, nothin'll happen." But it wasn't like that.

When you mind your own business, people'll think that you a sucker, and they'll try to step to you, tryin' to take your money or tryin' to take this: "Gimme your book bag, gimme your sneakers." And I'm be like, "Yo, I ain't givin' you shit!" And then they see that total attitude in you, they be like, "Yo. I'm a put dis guy on his ass." If they try to hit me, I hit 'em back, and then we gonna be fightin' . . . for what? 'Cause he wanted to take my book bag. But meanwhile, it wasn't me that was lookin' fuh the trouble; it was the other kid.

You know what was the real thing that got me? My moms took me out of Morris, and a month later, some kids got shot up in the park that I used to walk through to get home from school. Did you hear about that? One

bullet hit right between the girl's eyes. That January, that's when those kids got lit up in the park. And it was over some guy asking this other guy, "Why you wit' my girl?" And the girl's like, "Me and you broke up. . . ." and he was like, "Awright." He left, he came back, they was still there, and he sprayed the whole place at about the same time I used to be walking by. So I'd a been right there in the mix wit' em, and I woulda caught a bullet. For what? Innocent bystander, you know wha' I'm sayin'? God forbid, I'd a been dead right now if my moms and me wouldn't a decided I needed a change.

How do I know I ain't gonna be one of them next, laid out in the corner? My block is bad. They were sellin' drugs, and my moms knew they was killin' people left and right. Every day, there was another body. I was twelve, thirteen when I started to be aware. One time, I was with my sisters in the park playin', and all I heard was, "Pah, pah, pah!" It was like, "Oh shit!" We all just jumped to the ground 'cause my pops, you know, he's a vet, he's like, "If you ever hear shots, jump to the floor." We seen two kids runnin'. So we went over to look wha' happened, because all the shots was gone, and they had shot up this old man. Maybe he did somethin' to dem, I don't know. But they just shot him up and left him right there.

Somebody might just come by and be lookin' for one person, and see that person in a crowd and spray the whole crowd. He'll kill six people to just try to get that one guy, and he might not even get him. It's kinda scary. We used to go to the pizza shop, and they used to sell drugs outta the shop. I never knew dat until they busted it. But we all used to chill there. One day I see the ambulance, and one of the guys from the shop is gettin' put into it. This guy, he used to hang wi' my brother, and he started sellin' drugs in this park right there. Crack. It was a Red Top spot [a location claimed by a specific dealer who sells only red-topped vials of crack] and he was sellin' other color tops on their territory. So they was like, "Yo, we gonna get dis fucker," and they caught him slippin'. He got blasted and left two babies behind.... He was seventeen or eighteen. That shit just woke all of us up. This ain't a game.

Not a lot of people wake up and try to help others unless it really happens to them. Which is true, 'cause that's how I first got into it. Like AIDS, I was, "Damn, forget about AIDS; I ain't tryin' to learn about AIDS. I ain't gonna catch it." Then one of my cousins wound up catchin' AIDS, and she died. That makes me think this is real, and it's takin' a lotta people down.

A person that grows up in that type environment, even with all this shit, they'll maybe still wanna be a drug dealer, because they see the drug dealers in the Lexus and the BMW, the nice cars, the nice jewelry and everything, wit' no jobs to show fuh none o' that. Sell cracks on the corner in fronta moms, pops; they didn't care who they'd sell in front of. Mad kids, young kids that just growin' up. Kids my age pushin' cracks for the crack house. Just dealin' drugs, but things is gonna break down; they gonna catch you sooner or later. Some guys, growin' up in there, they see dis guy get arrested for dealin' an' seen the guy was makin' a lotta money, so they'll try to take over the spot. Meanwhile there's somebody else tryin' to take over the spot, so they gonna get killt. It's gonna be a conflic' back and forth, for what? Over the concrete that doesn't belong to nobody but the city. You know wha' I'm sayin'?

## Coming to Satellite Academy

I knew Satellite was a different type of school, 'cause my sister was attendin' it at the time I was in Morris. Since she had been going to Satellite, I noticed that she had changed. She had more respec' for herself in general. Before, she would curse, argue, be a big mouth in fronta anybody; she didn't care. I was in my freshman year at Morris and I was, "Yo. This school must be right 'cause she's calmer now. She just be chillin', and she can help me wit' my work because now she understands it."

So I applied and did the interview and got in, and the school told me, "Look, this school is not like a regular school. Nobody's gonna start trouble wit' you, 'cause if there's a fight in the school, you kicked out, regardless of the matter, whether he hit you first and you hit him back. Ya'll both outta here." It really made me think, "Damn, I ain't tryin' to get into a fight, 'cause I wanna do what I gotta do. I wanna get out a school, go to college maybe, and achieve some of the goals that I'm tryin' to achieve." So I was like, "Look, I'm just gonna maintain this chill."

It was a whole different setting, and it was difficult in a way, because sometimes somebody would get on your nerves. They'll say stupid stuff, or they'll try to snap on you. I just tried to tell them to calm down. That was my favorite words, "Yo, calm down." They would tell you they were calm, but their voice be screamin' at you. They'd get me so pumped where I'd go over to th' teacher . . . 'cause that what they tell us to do: go over to a teacher and tell him that you wanna get mediated. So one time I got mediated with this girl, and we settled our differences. We just left it to the side.

With schoolwork at Satellite, it was, "Oh, you don't understand? Let's take a look." They really helped you to try to understand. They puts more attention on students as individuals. At first I was slackin' off, but the teachers came back to me, "Look, I got a proposition for you. Do this, a little bit extra here, and you will get credit." I was like, "Mm . . . sounds good." They did that for me, they looked out, they help you to learn. I did all the work I was supposed to do. I'm even tryin' to get my cousin in here.

▲ *Phil in the classroom (above)*

## Becoming a Conflict-Resolution Mediator

The only reason I took Tony's conflict-resolution class is 'cause I needed the writing credit. I thought Tony and the class was gonna be a drag. Then towards the middle of the semester, I started to enjoy it and came to believin' maybe conflict resolution could work. That it could help you get yourself outta problems that maybe you couldn't handle before.

I started changing. I felt calmer, 'cause before, I was ready to fight, right away, and there was no turnin' back from that. But I started to look at conflic' in a totally different way. At first I was disagreein' wi' what Tony was

tellin' me, because he was sayin' that the conflict resolution'll work outside of the classroom and school. And I was like, "Yo, that shit ain't never gonna work outside a school. Maybe in the school, but not outside of the school." Until Tony just started us doin' more research, on the Bloods and the Crips and all that, and on Gandhi.

Gandhi—he was a leader. He wanted no violence, and yet his people still insisted on killin' people, because they figured that that was the only way. But he tol' 'em that he ain't gonna eat till they stop the violence. He didn't eat, and they stopped. That was wild, man, 'cause he was willin' to starve hisself, just so people will stop

their fightin', and they believed in him so much. Gandhi, yeah, he did his thing. You know what I'm sayin'?

Tony is a mad cool person, you know. He'll do a lotta stuff to keep you into the game, like we did this go-around on picking the color of conflict. The majority of the people was red, you know, bloodshed. Just about everybody in the class has seen somebody get killed or, you know, has family or a friend killed. One girl, she picked black, white, blue, and red. She said when the black man and the white man get together, they cause bloodshed, and then the cops get in and lock up the black man. That shit was mad deep. He'll do role-playing, and we act it out so real that it makes you get into it real. It makes your mind just start thinkin' in all different types of ways, like how to make a positive decision. And we started just goin' deep in the past, and how it worked for others. So I was like, "Damn, it does work."

But it's up to you, if you wanna put it to work, how to solve problems creatively. All that had me interested in the class and kept me goin'. At Morris—well, back then, really I didn't think there was a different way to settle things. 'Cause, you know, lotta people did it the same way, just fighting, and if you was any different, you was either a oddball or a sucka. Now I feel that there could have been another way. I could have avoided alla dat, just by talkin' to the person. Before I took the class, there was no such thing as, "Well, let's talk about this." And really back then, I don't think I could've talked things out. I didn't know how to handle it. It woulda come out wrong to the person, and then we woulda made it a bigger problem than what it was. But now I feel dat communication is the main key, right there.

The word *communication* to me now means when two parties can hold a conversation without gettin' violent, not raisin' they voice. That way, they can take in each other's ideas and really look deep into it. If I bump this person, I'll tell him, "Look, I didn't mean to do that, I'm sorry." But sometimes it just slips your mind, or sometimes you just be at the point where you be like, "Fuck dis." But you just gotta maintain, keep your head up, and do what you gotta do. I know if I don't, somethin' is gonna hit me in the long run, not physically, but mentally. It's gonna smack me in the face, and I'm a be like, "Damn, why didn't I do that the right way?"

It's all about looks these days, y'know. "Oh, you looked at me wrong, and now we ready to fight." From there, I'll punch you, you punch me, then somebody gotta come back wit' a gun, then from the gun it escalate to murder, from murder to twenty-five years in jail. For what? Over a look—over, "Oh, you looked at me wrong; that's why I shot you." Come on, man, that's stupid. And all this respect stuff. "Oh, you disrespect me, I'm a get you, I'm come see you." That's basically what it is. Now when a person'll look at me all hard, I just kind of laugh it off, not at him, but at the situation. In the past, it would've been like, "What the fuck you lookin' at?" Excuse the expression—I woulda' said some shit, get everybody amped up, and then they woulda just went up to the fifth floor from there. 'Cause we was lookin' at each other.

There's always somebody out there that's gonna test you to see if you are the hard rock that you think you are. That's exactly what they do, but it's all fear. They'll look at you real hard, and they think by lookin' at you hard, tha' you jus' gonna back down, because they so scared that you wouldn't. It's like a transaction, you know wha' I'm sayin'? It's that fear, back 'n' forth from both parties. What else is going on is anger. There's some kids that just need help, because their parents are just messed up.

I had a friend, you know the lady I showed you, that's his aunt, and she's smoking crack. His pops died when he was like three, and dat's what hurt him the most, because even though he was livin' wit' his mom, his moms didn't care about him. Never used to give him shit. He was always hustlin'. Doin' somethin', like shovelin' snow when it snowed, or selling crack. He had no other choice, 'cause he was too young to get a legal job. That was like one of the main reasons why he was the way he was. Some people will mentally abuse him, tell him, "Oh, you ain't worth nothin'." They'll make him feel so bad, that the next person that says anything to him, period, he's gonna wanna beat him up. That's the only way he knew how to handle his problems. He figured he ain't have nobody to defend him, both mentally and physically.

Some people that have been neglected all their life by their moms and pops, they b'like, "Fuck it, I ain't got nothin' else to live for." That's how peoples think. So, someone is gonna get blasted. It's like they get attention from it. You know, by writin' on this wall, by beatin' up this kid, dissin' this person. All this just to get attention. But they need more lovin', lovin' attention, you know wha' I'm sayin, and then they'll b'like, "Damn, you know, there's somebody that really does love me out 'dere."

In Tony's class I did a couple of example mediations, and I felt that they gonna need somebody else to help the new students. So I became a mediator. I hit the new ones in the head. You know, be like, "Yo, this how it's goin' down. Everybody repec' yo; you respect them. If you got a problem, you come see me, or you come see somebody else to mediate, and we'll handle it. Y'know wha' I'm sayin'? Don't try to handle it yourself. I'm not sayin' you can't handle it, but it's like leavin' an apple on the table for a week; it's gonna turn rotten. So, you gotta just let someone else handle it. Let someone else cut it up."

I thought I would be good at it, 'cause I'm good wit' people. I'll make people laugh in the mediation. Like if I'm sittin' down wit' these two angry-assed people wit' faces like bulldogs, I'm gonna try to make them laugh, but be takin' it serious to do the job. I be like, "Yo, why you doin' this? 'Cause you was lookin' at him, and he was lookin' at you? Ya'll bof ugly, anyway!" Ask them the questions we was taught, get 'em goin', you know. I'll explain it to them, my point of view, like, "Yo, for what was alla this? Over she took your book or she took your seat in class? Get another seat. Know wha' I'm sayin'? Avoid dat problem. By now you coulda been learnin' that algebra that you missed out on, and you could be passin' that test you got the next day. But instead you're in here, with me."

## Solutions

I think it would be appropriate for every school to have mediation and conflict resolution. And I know it'll turn out better than what a lotta people think. It'll help keep people out on the streets, as well as inside the schools, to maintain themselves. Approach a person the proper way insteada the wrong way. On a real-to-real basis, like, "Yo, this is how it is, this is how I feel, da-da-da. . . ." If he has any feedback on like what I told him, by all means, do that, too. Stop this miscommunication. I got this chance now with Tony to maybe talk at other schools about mediation, and I think I cou' do it. It'll be good to spread my knowledge. Just keep it real with them, straight-up basis with them, no half-steppin' or nothin'.

I know some will be like I was and won't think it'll work. But I'll be like, "Sit down, man, let me talk to you for a minute." Then I'll break down some examples that I went through. And if he's willin' to learn, and let's say he been through practically the same shit I have been through, he'll understand my point. So I'll be like, "Look, you know wha' happened wi' me? That was the same thing I used to say. But believe you me, when you get

into a problem, you'll never know until you try it."

I know it helped me. I know I'm not totally nonviolent now, but it just really opened my eyes, and that's all you need to do to a person. Open they eyes to the real world. Let them know that some peers are gettin' killed over the stupidest problems—"you lookin' at me wrong, you stepped on my sneakers"—and then you get a pop. But I'll also let 'em know that it's hard to maintain, because sometimes it is. But it works, even out on the street. Whatever you do comes back to you. Like, I'm not tryin' to be funny, but if I help this old lady across the street,

maybe somebody's helpin' my grandmother across the street somewhere in Puerto Rico, even tho' I'm not there. In the long run, you get it back.

One bad person, livin' around where I live, doesn't make everyone bad. But if we get one person from every block in New York, just one person, understanding conflict resolution, it'll make a difference. 'Cause that one person knows people on the block, and if they see a person getting into a problem, they'll tell this person, "Yo, look, why you tryin' to even get into this, man? Don't even worry about that. You gonna get stressed. Don't try to get your life taken over some stupid shit." It takes a man to say somethin', to talk. You know wha' I'm sayin'?

▲ *Graduation (above)*

PHIL and ANTONIO

# ANTONIO

I be that rubber, put it on 'er, lay-tex the best maneuver
Ghetto life's the game we play and I don't want to be a loser
Yo there's so many ways to go, plenty ways to die
I want to stay alive not to get caught by HIV stupidity
So why get got with that
When the smartest thing to do is just throw on your jimmy hat
Informed is to be warned, so the rapper may be torn
Yo that be my word is born, like the condom gets thrown on
*Yo no quiero mirar en la cara del sida*
*Si no te cuida te quita la vida*
I'm not a dope slinger smacked out needle
Pop 'er a raw American, thanks to my Latin Mama
*La muerte llama a todos que no saben y los bobos y tontos que no usan el condón*
So it be that Black bro' with that Yasir Arafat flow
It's time to smash those lies and blow 'em out like nappy Afros
Am I the one to judge the ethics and the values
Get the STD, get honey-roasted like a cashew
So forget how it feels, protect the coochie and the dills
BX youth in action, keeping it real

## Straight-up Funk

I was eight when I moved to 174th Street. The only reason my mother really got that apartment was because my uncle's wife got two apartments at the same time, and she only needed one, so we moved into the other. But my uncle started smokin' crack, so my aunt and him broke up, and that apartment, where we lived, she wanted it back. So we left and went to live in the apartment with my uncle, and he was a crackhead at that time.

Living with my uncle, it was definitely an experience I wasn't used to. It was weird. Now that I think about it, it was like a dark place, a gloomy-type dark. I would come into the house, and the kitchen'll be bright, but the livin' room, that was my uncle's space. You could just sense that somethin' wasn't right there. It was just dark, and there was an odor, a funk, it was a straight-up funk. 'Cause my uncle, he did not take a bath. Then, also, maybe it could be like a spiritual thing like, you know,

bad odors and bad deeds bring in evil spirits. So a funk in that sense—the vibe.

That was nasty to come into, every day after school. I was like twelve, goin' on thirteen. There was lotta conflict between my uncle and my mother. He used to steal. He stole like an air conditioner and a lotta figurines. My parents was always scared to leave, because they knew when they came back that everything could be gone from the house. And my father's like, "Oh, I don't wanna hurt this man." My mother's goin' through troubles. Another reason she moved there was because she wanted to help him. She wanted to be a nice sister, and he's her only real brother.

When you're younger, you think that you know a lot. But I was still pretty much innocent at that time. I knew he was a crackhead, and that he stunk, but I guess I was just basically livin' through it. I really didn't have a choice. Him and my mother's relationship was never, ever the same. They used to be real close, but for like a couple a years my mother didn't speak to him. Because of the conflict between him and my mother, it almost made my mother and father break up. We moved outta there quick, because it just caused too much turbulence all throughout the house.

After that I moved to Walton Avenue, and that was like real close to the other buildin' I lived in before my uncle. I was in junior high school at the time, so I was goin' back to where I used to live, and that's when I started, you know, gettin' more into the dark side of life. I started venturing out on my own, going far, learning about girls, and learning more about street activities. I wasn't a homebody anymore; I was hanging out widda lot of my friends and things like that.

You know what? When I was nine or ten years old, I used to pack bags in supermarkets, and you know what's funny about it? The same guys I worked with packing bags, later on, we was to do bad things together. We all used to work at that store to make money, insteada robbin' people an' sellin' drugs, and then it's like we all changed at the same time. Let me see if I could put it in a nutshell: In the beginning, we was just hanging out. It was fun, and it was different. Not to put fun and negativity in the same place, 'cause there was a lot of negative things goin' on around that area. Wanting money, selling drugs, and bein' around guns. Carryin' guns all the time, and not really havin' a positive outlook on life. Only if you have fat pockets, a lot of jewelry, an' a lot of women around you; you're thinking that's the only way you gonna have a good life.

There was a lot crackheads around, and robbin', fights, shootings, and a lot of, let me see, peer pressure. We definitely didn't know any better. We really didn't think about the consequences. The pain that we could cause other people—I wasn't thinkin' about it. I was so drunk and so high most of the time that I never thought about it. We was basically selfish, just thinkin' about ourselves. Just livin' for today. Really, it seemed natural to do the selling and to rob people. It was an everyday experience. I thought that was the way everybody and every-

thing was. I just didn't have enough knowledge of self or enough knowledge of anything to pull myself outta that. Now I know that there was other things that I coulda done, that it wasn't the only way out or to survive. But at that point, you don't know that much about life.

I didn't really get to see other people doing anything positive. I really didn't know who I was, or where I stood in society. I just thought I was gonna be a drug dealer, for the . . . To tell you the truth, I used to get into so much trouble that I thought somebody was gonna kill me before I turned eighteen. I didn't have a place. I was a follower. It was also a feelin', like now I'm a man; I could make my own decisions, I knew everything that life had to offer, and I felt that everything I was doin' was right. So, every decision I made was narrow, because my vision hadn't been widened yet. I was only doin' the things that I knew, which was a lotta negative things. But I was tryin' to do it to the best of my ability, so you know I was screwin' up big time [laughing]. I was good at it. It's like I thought I knew it all.

Around when I first started high school, I was havin' problems with my parents. My father at one point said, "This is not my son. This is a totally different person." I would just smoke pot, not go to school, and drink beer every day. Every dollar that we got went to this. That's basically what my life revolved around at that point.

## Spotford and Change

This type of activity, at its heaviest, went on for about three years, 'cause then I went to Spotford [a juvenile detention center]. I was in a cab, and I got caught with a gun on me, so the judge said, "There you go." Yeah, there I go, and there I went, to Spotford. I went there for

▲ *Antonio speaking in class (above)*

like a week, but that week made me not wanna go in there again. I didn't have any freedom, 'cause they tell you what time to take a shower, what to eat. I was like, "Man, I wanna go outside." I had a couple a laughs in there, saw people I knew. Nothin' really scared me, but it was just the whole scenario; it was like, "I can't see myself in here when I'm twenty-five, doin' seven years. What am I doin' with my life?" I only did a week, and it gave me a chance to reflect.

After that time, I noticed myself starting to change. I didn't wanna be in that situation anymore. I knew that

wasn't me. I was thinkin' about this on the train today; there's other guys that been through the same thing I been through, but, I thought, "What makes me different from them? What makes me wanna leave that life, and what makes them wanna stay in it?" I really don't know, but I know Spotford definitely had something to do with it. I used to think it was probably cool to go to jail, because when other guys that went to jail came home, they got a lot a respect. They said, "Yeah, I was a big man there; I had people washin' my drawers." But the reality is that jail is not a joke. It's not a lifestyle that I choose to live.

I put myself in a lotta dangerous situations where I

probably shouldn't even be here right now speakin'. I definitely thank God and my parents; they musta done something right. To tell you the truth, I feel that I never really had it that hard. My parents pretty much gave me everything I wanted, but I think it was the excitement behind the other stuff, or just being ignorant to what I was really doin'. Actually, throughout most of my life, I've been very selfish. I guess you could call it spoiled, in the sense where I didn't think about other people's feelings. I always wanted to do what I wanna do.

My self-worth, that was really a struggle. I guess I got the idea from people I was hangin' out with that I would need money to get the girls, to get the car, to get anything I wanted. I would look and see that I didn't have anything I wanted, and then I would blame the lack of money on my parents, because they didn't have any money to give me. A lotta times, I used to be depressed because I wouldn't have any currency, and I didn't wanna go outside to stick anybody up. So I would just stay home, feelin' sorry for myself, and thinkin' about the things that I didn't have. My mother'd be like, "Come on, son, I don't like to see you like this. Try to tell me what's goin' on." But the relationship between my parents and me was, like, blocked.

I could never really communicate with them that well. I found myself alone a lot of the times, dealin' with a lotta things by myself. But my mother and father, they always asked me, "Come on, tell us what's goin' on. We wanna help you." I never really opened up to them, but throughout all my troubles and my good times, my parents always been there to give me some type of support. Also, I see they always work hard for what they get, and they always told me that the reason that I never really ap-

preciate a lotta things is because I didn't have to earn them myself.

After Spotford, I went back to Alfred E. Smith High School. Even after I came outta Spotford, it still took me a while to leave the people I was hangin' with, to actually stop and to not go out every time I didn't have any money, to stop sellin' the drugs and not rob people. I was havin' nightmares, and I was just really scared. I felt like I needed some guidance. My parents were tryin' to help me, but I guess it had to be outside guidance. I started seekin' help at Alfred E. Smith, and it started when I trusted a woman named Miss Williams. She was the head of my house at school, and somehow I got attached to her and just started speakin' to her. I guess to her I portrayed two different people, or I had two different lifestyles. I just started openin' up to her slowly, and one day I asked her a question: I said, "Miss Williams, you think I'm a good guy, you know?" Her answer was, "Yeah!" I was like, "Nah, no, I'm not." Then she looked at me kinda strange, and I guess she musta heard my cry for help.

I don't remember exactly what we spoke about, but I know I probably told her about a couple of the things that I was doin' out in the street, and she recommended a counselor to me. I opened up right away to him. I guess I really needed someone to talk to, 'cause I really didn't beat around the bush too much. I wanted some help. We would meet three or four times a week. Around then, the school said that I wouldn't be able to graduate from there in time, so they told me I had to go. And I told my counselor, and he referred me to Bronx Satellite.

After I had been in Satellite, I didn't see my old counselor for almost two years. When he came to visit me, he was shocked, because he told me he had never seen so much emotion come outta me. Most of our conversations in the past, I guess, musta been real rugged and to the point. Even though I would tell him things, I guess the way that I told him was just not that emotional. I really didn't know then if I was gonna change or not. I didn't really change until I got here to Satellite.

## The Journey Begins

Once I got here, I really started to slow down sellin' weed. I guess the main reason was because of the two best friends that I used to do all my dirt with, all my activities—one was in jail and the other one got married and started a little family. There were still times in Satellite where I was into sellin' weed for the money, just for the money, but real changes started to happen to me there. Not only did I want to change, but there was people there helpin' me, teaching me things to help me to change, and just givin' me a different aspect on things. I didn't wanna live in that kind of life anymore. . . . I didn't wanna be a criminal. To be the best criminal, you either gotta be real intelligent or just crazy. And I don't know which category I fitted in.

Plus, I started to see the suffering that I was putting my mother through: her comin' to see me in court, and my parents gettin' into arguments because of me. I guess I wanted to be a good son. I wanted to be a good guy. But it is hard to change and leave that old way behind, 'cause you still in the same environment. It was still easy for me to get peer-pressured, and I still didn't have a definition of myself yet. Plus the negativity still attracted me an enormous amount. I was smokin' a lotta weed. Even though I wanted to change, one person'd be like, "Come on, we gonna go smoke and rhyme." So, it was like,

"Damn, now I have to make a choice," and I would just leave and go with them. I definitely still had the same mentality, and I wasn't strong enough yet to say no, I guess. Maybe I wasn't ready, or maybe I figured that I still had some time for just takin' life as a joke.

The people that you do all those things with, you become close. In a way, they become like your family. It's hard to just break that bond you all have, and now I see that, to a certain extent, the bond that had us was the criminal life. But it got to the point where it was just too much trouble. One time, this guy came to my door to get a bag of weed, and then he didn't want to pay me, and this is right at my front door. My father's right in the livin' room, and he doesn't know that I'm doin' this. I was gettin' ready to either get my bag, get my money, or we was gonna go at it to see who comes out victorious. I was gonna catch a body—but then I was like, four hundred dollars, my freedom, his life? I had to balance out which was more important, and that was really the last deal I did. I just had to stop.

It's a violent lifestyle; it's unsympathetic; a shark-type lifestyle; a predator, kill-or-be-killed instinct; a total mind-state; and I don't want to live like that. I just didn't want to put myself through that. Maybe it's the self-worth part that I didn't even know I had. But I'm worth more than bein' in jail. I just decided to get out of it completely.

What helped me at Satellite was the truthfulness and the bluntness. Everybody could be themselves, and they'll accept you for who you are and try to work with you. They try to build self-esteem. Tryin' to push out your in-di-vi-du-a-li-ty, and also to help you to work with a group. I definitely feel that this school gave me a boost in a different type of knowledge—human knowledge, not just scholastic knowledge. I think the lack of human knowledge and self-education is why things are the way they are around my area. We're missing something, and that's makin' us act self-destructive. Maybe it's also the things that we do have that make us self-destructive, 'cause you think about it, what do we really have? We have crack on one corner, and a liquor store on the other. Those are a way to escape, and plus, once you all drunk and high, you're not thinkin' straight anyway. Most likely, you gonna go out there an' do somethin' crazy, like kill your brother. It may be pride, like if somebody steps on your shoes or bumps you. You feel they tryin' to play you to do somethin' back to them, like kill them. There's many fights I've been in, just because people look at me wrong, and I'm just being ignorant. Sometimes it's just wanting to take your anger out on anybody, so you just do it any way you can, and it come down to killin', and a-stabbin' and a-shootin'.

I didn't take the conflict-resolution course, but just bein' around the idea helps. It's definitely affected me in a really positive way. Just findin' out that, if you think about it and you dwell on it hard enough, you probably will always find another way out of a tight situation. Maybe just knowing that you can walk away, you don't have to get into it, and that you have a choice. Like when I see people arguing, "Please, don't fight, Brothers and Sisters [laughing]. Let's all love each other. We don't need to resort to violence." Even jokingly, it sticks with you, and I apply it.

## Changing Roles and New Truths

I have two pretty big positions in the school. Sometimes I don't wanna be in those positions, because it's too much responsibility. But then again, I do, because it gives

me a chance to play a different role in school and in my life. Like bein' more responsible, 'cause I don't consider myself that much of a responsible person. Sometimes I just put things on hold. So I felt it would definitely help me and make me a better person; that's really the reason I did it.

One position is being a Senior Pioneer, in the very first Senior Pioneer class. We make portfolios of our work, and we also help come up with new methods that other classes behind us could follow about how to graduate, instead of just passing those tests and havin' those little scores and transcripts to prove how smart you are. Maybe this way they find out who you are, and not just that you know what they want you to know.

Another role that I have is being a student teacher. As a student teacher, I'm learning how to run a class, facilitate a class, and help a teacher out with her work. Even though it might be a little petty sometimes, like stapling worksheets or things like that, I feel it's a good experience for me. People, they be like, "Oh, Antonio, can you help me with this? I don't know how to do this." At first I wasn't gonna take that class, because I know I still have so many things to work on. Also I knew it was gonna be a lotta work, so I was playin' my lazy role. But I ended up learnin' a lotta things. It showed me that I could be a leader and teach people without anybody else around. It taught me teamwork; I worked with five other assistants. And it taught me that with hard work and planning, you can accomplish a lot.

It's funny, then and now I need a lotta support to do things, because somethin' in my mind makes me maybe not wanna accomplish the things that I could do. I'm like that with everything in life. As soon as it start gettin' hard, I quit, and you know how the sayin' goes, "No pain, no gain." So, now I'm startin' to learn for myself to just go through the struggle, because it'll be worthwhile.

## Learning His History

What helped me a lot was learning about my history, African-American history. Basically how people had to struggle way more than I did, and if they could do it, I could also. How life wasn't always like this, and our people didn't always kill each other in the streets over nonsense. That there was a time when we actually stuck together and made things possible. Especially readin' about Malcolm X gave me self-esteem. He did way more things than I did, and it made me feel that I could accomplish things. But it also made me feel another struggle.

Before, my struggle was havin' the money, being popular, and now I could see them as minor things, petty. But then, when I started watchin' films and readin' books and gettin' ideas in Laura's class, that's one of the first times I could really remember seeing strong images. Like learning about Malcolm X and wantin' to make a positive statement. I really felt proud that people could not be concerned only about themselves. It was something that I always wanted, but I just never got the chance to see it. Watchin' Malcolm X and readin' the book made me approach life in a totally different way, and I think I was ready for that.

I personally feel that it's the level of consciousness that a person is ready to accept and has been around. Because if Malcolm never went to Mecca, he woulda never been around that consciousness, and when he saw the truth, he had no choice but to accept it and adapt it into his life, which is something like I did. I saw the truth and had no choice but to adapt it in my life. I could no longer live in that minor fairy tale. When I read the book, I was like, "Damn, fuckin' white people, how can they do that?" But then, with the more classes that I took, I realized maybe it really wasn't their fault, that was just their cultures and their traditions, and they happen to bring it upon our people. I just started lookin' at human beings, I mean, white and black, and yellow, whatever, as not a color, but as human beings and just different cultures and religions. That helped me wanna bring people together, insteada havin' that separatism, when we need to get down with the human race. But some of us just fail to realize that. I can identify with Malcolm X and Martin Luther King, Frederick Douglass, W. E. B. Du Bois, and Harriet Tubman, because they all wanted better for their people. They started, you know, from the sole of the shoe and worked it all the way up to the tip of the head.

A lotta people do know the truth, but some people just reject it and keep on livin' the fantasy life of materialism. They fail to realize that the real struggle we as human beings are having now is tryin' to live together. Tryin' to save this world long enough for our great-great-grandchildren to live in it. A struggle to raise consciousness; to try to accept people for who they are, and not be prejudiced, racist, or sexist. Tryin' to help others, which a lot of us don't do today, 'cause everybody thinks about themselves.

A lotta the trouble I used to get in back then was because of my ego. I used to think that I knew it all, that I was stronger than everybody, that nobody could beat me,

*Working on a neighborhood development project* ▶

that I'm invincible. A lotta people have that ego problem today. They like, "Oh, because I got these clothes on and these shoes on, I'm better." Once you think that way, it reflects on how you act and the things you do, so it becomes a whole cycle. And when other people help you live up to that, to that name, the more reinforcement you get to thinkin' that it's right.

One of the things that makes strong, powerful leaders and helps change people's lives is caring. The way I see it, we have to change not only the way the people think, but help them to realize certain things about themselves. Then soon you won't be the only person taking action.

That's exactly what's happenin' in my buildin'. I live in a nice buildin', but it's startin' to go to the dogs, because the same people that live in there are messin' it up. But by our actions to keep the buildin' together, we are the ones that set an example for them.

Basically, our communities need more leaders, more young leaders. If you followin' peer pressure, you're not being a leader. A leader doesn't necessarily mean that you have to be the leader of a country, but just to lead yourself. To know yourself and walk your own path without really wantin' to follow behind anybody's footsteps, unless they're positive steps. Insteada just makin' a park or a basketball court, which is good, also make a place where you could make leaders. From there, it'll just be a domino effect. Like with the lot we cleaned out and made the garden for the class. We did it, and it was real positive.

If we talk about leadership in the communities, we have to talk about responsibility, and that is a major, ma-

*Antonio speaking with Carol—at graduation* ▶

jor word and probably the thing that a lot of us lack. Responsibility is what gives a person worth and dignity. Responsibility is a value, meaning to be responsible for a life, or even knowin' that every action has a reaction. If you become responsible for your actions, you'll change a whole lot. You will think before you do things. So many people don't hold themselves responsible for things. All of this, your whole entire book, should pro'ly be called responsibility.

I realize that maybe in other parts of the world, kids our age, you know, they have a harder struggle. I definitely see that I am in a part of the world where I could accomplish a lotta things. One of my main goals is to be recognized in the way of revolutionary change. The way I see it, it'll start very small, and it starts from myself. We was talkin' about responsibility; I gotta take responsibility to actually commit to myself, to slowly make those changes and start accomplishing things so I can feel better about myself.

I know that everybody gotta live their life, and things happen. But to live your life, you accept those things and stay focused on what you wanna do, what you wanna change, and actually start doin' it, insteada talkin' about it. I realize that this is a life we live every single day of the three hundred and sixty-five, then every hour, every minute, every second. We do have a lotta things that happens around us; it does affect us. 'Cause life will be a struggle sometimes; you even gotta fight to come out your mother's womb. But even though something could have rubbed you the wrong way, take it upon yourself to be stronger than that, and still do what you got to do. It's as simple as that.

## TONY SCHWAB / conflict-resolution teacher

Of course it would be worthwhile to teach conflict resolution in all schools, but Gandhi or King is not everybody's cup of tea. I would venture a guess that since Reagan was a lot of people's cup of tea, as was the Gulf War, even people who call themselves liberal are used to a fight and used to a struggle, sometimes to the death. I think a lot of people are scared of the Gandhian outlook, which is that everybody is moral enough to be kind. I think that most of us believe that we're not good enough to be kind; we've gotta fight, scrap, and save our own selves.

Schools are a lot about behavior and behavior modification; intellectual behavior modification. Learning your history; learning your reading and writing, . . . and learning how to sit in the seat. Schools don't want to say, "I

▲ *Antonio with Tony Schwab (above)*

want to teach kids how to open up and be alive, and how to teach love. Do I wanna teach love?" Everybody didn't like the hippies, either, and now there's a whole revamping of history, to put the hippies off to one side and bring Nixon and his White House up. The sixties are getting rewritten. And, therefore, it's sorta easy for people to say, "No, thank you. We'll teach them reading and writing." And what they call "thinking," which can have some beautiful results, to be able to be a good thinker.

But what we teach in this school, and what our students want to learn, is how to live your life so that you can be confident you're gonna be around tomorrow. I think a lot of the more well-to-do people, including the teachers in our system, think this is not a problem; they will be around tomorrow. They're not as worried as some of us, that the idea of a good future, of a happy future, is being tampered with. So in a way, we're antiestablishment.

The establishment is prone to violence, and it's prone to pride. It's prone to focusing on number one, or number two. We go, and we say, "If you're number fifty, you've still got a helluva lot goin' for you."

The problem with our society that I'm starting to see is that all the stuff it holds out to us to do, the requirements—reading, writing, and arithmetic—buy you a life. They help you exist. They get you food on your table. So who's gonna laugh at that? What I realized is that when they offer you food for being what they call literate, or computer-literate, that's a big incentive. Because all my kids and me are lookin' for food. And for a lifestyle.

But what they're also doing, like Antonio says, is putting blinders on your view of this other, deeper reality of living, which is to be kind to one another and to change society together for the better, because we all are lookin' out for each other. That would be better than just doling out jobs and food to people if they can pass certain tests. But it takes a commitment, and it also takes people's eyes being opened. That does not happen because I tell you to open your eyes. It happens because your eyes *get* opened. Yeah, I wish that I had a machine that could do it. But the only machine around that I see to open eyes is life itself: experiences, poetry, art, conversation, example, reading, and crisis.

What I teach, and what these kids are now able to teach, is not just for them. It's exactly what the doctor ordered for everybody. The people who think they have it made, or who are only worried about losing a sixty-thousand-dollar-a-year job—they're hiding. They don't know that they need the same things I need, and the same things my students need. They need a sense of peace, and a sense that life will be kind to them, because they love themselves and because they are looking out for other people. If my students could feel that somebody who thinks they have it made was looking out for them, and that somebody could feel that they were being looked out for by my students, then the world would start to equal out.

We gotta open up this wound. And this wound is that we all, in a way, you could say, hate each other. Because we're all hurting so much. And we're all so worried about ourselves and our families, because of the legitimate threats all around us, that we forget our neighbors have the exact same feelings we do. The exact same problems, and the exact same fear of death, and fear of bankruptcy. If we unplugged from the system that's got us so freaked out, and scared, and busy—I think busyness is a real problem in our culture—then we would be able to look at one another and help one another. I don't want us all to go around singing folk songs together and holding hands—no! We've got to really love one another. We've got to really be there for one another. And I don't have enough time to do it, in my life, so I know there's other people who don't have time either. And my kids, the students here, have started to take the time, to see that life is more than the struggle for the next buck.

**JUDY SCOTT** / principal, Schomberg Bronx Satellite Academy

Schomberg Satellite Academy is an alternative public high school for students who have left the large, traditional schools for a new start. We offer an opportunity for young people to transform failure and defeat into confidence and triumph. This is a place where "you can't" becomes "I will." It is a place where time and attention is paid to the individual student as a person ready to make a positive change, as a scholar and a member of a community.

At present, we have two hundred students and sixteen

staff members. Students who apply to our school take a series of reading, writing, and math placement tests and are interviewed by students and staff who talk to them about making a commitment—to learning, sharing, and growing in a community.

Our school is honored to be named for Arturo A. Schomberg, a man who fought for independence for his native Puerto Rico and was a writer, political activist, and archivist for African-American history and culture as part of the Harlem Renaissance. We are located in the South Bronx, and our students are mostly young African-Americans and Latinos from the neighborhood, one of the most economically depressed areas of the country. Their family lives and educational careers have been assaulted by the demons of late-twentieth-century ghetto life in America: drugs; sudden and violent death; AIDS and chronic debilitating illness like asthma and TB; unemployment or minimum-wage jobs that lead nowhere; the hopeful, yet demanding daily attention required by children raised by grandmothers, or by mothers who are children themselves; racism and isolation—from sources of power and money, from those who have found a way out.

Our goal is to prepare students for college and meaningful careers. And it is equally important that our students learn how to create and maintain a community that values creativity, achievement, intellectual and social challenges, understanding, and the peaceful resolution of conflicts. We talk about these goals in class and learn how to achieve them in our work and our relationship with one another. We make connections with families and community groups who are making the South Bronx a place of hope and promise.

▲ *With Judy Scott (above)*

PHIL and ANTONIO

# About the Author

ANTHONY ALLISON is a professional photographer, documentarian, human rights advocate, and youth counselor who has worked closely with Jimmy Carter and the Carter Center and is currently co-director of Hoops for Hope (www.hoopsafrica.org). He lives in New York City. This is his first book.